MAINERS ON THE *TITANIC*

MAINERS ON THE *TITANIC*

Mac Smith

Camden, Maine

Published by Down East Books
An imprint of Rowman & Littlefield
4501 Forbes Boulevard, Suite 200, Lanham, Maryland 20706
www.rowman.com

10 Thornbury Road, Plymouth PL6 7PP, United Kingdom

Distributed by National Book Network
Copyright © 2014 by Malcolm Smith

British Library Cataloguing in Publication Information Available

Library of Congress Cataloging-in-Publication Data

Smith, Malcolm, 1964-
Mainers on the Titanic / Malcolm Smith.
pages cm
Includes bibliographical references.
ISBN 978-1-60893-304-4 (pbk. : alk. paper) -- ISBN 978-1-60893-305-1 (electronic)
1. Titanic (Steamship) 2. Shipwrecks--North Atlantic Ocean. 3. Shipwreck victims--Maine--Biography. 4. Shipwreck victims--North Atlantic Ocean--Biography. 5. Maine--Biography. I. Title.
G530.T6S625 2014
910.9163'4--dc23
2014009465

♾™ The paper used in this publication meets the minimum requirements of American National Standard for Information Sciences Permanence of Paper for Printed Library Materials, ANSI/NISO Z39.48-1992.

Printed in the United States of America

This book is dedicated to Gram Ellis, Ma, and everyone else in my family. Love you much.

I

A lurking fear remained of possible bad tidings to come.
—*Bangor Daily Commercial*

In the wee hours of the morning of April 15, 1912, more than one hundred years ago, a group of Mainers were living a story that was so unlike any other that it continues to live on today. Some of those stories, much like the people who lived them, are famous, some not so famous; some are lost to history, some, nearly lost. The stories that came from the Maine passengers that horrible morning had one common theme, however: They were all utterly tragic.

Back home in Maine, on the same day the *Titanic* sank, that Monday morning started out quite differently. Enjoying the fresh spring weather, looking forward to Easter and the eventual arrival of their families and neighbors, people read the early articles contained in the state's newspaper excitedly but with a certain sense of relief. TITANIC STRIKES ICEBERG—ASSISTANCE IS ASKED FOR read the headline of the *Lewiston Daily Sun*'s April 15 morning edition, the article continuing with: "The last report was that she was sinking by the head and the women were being put off in lifeboats. Among the passengers were the Astors, Vanderbilts, and Wideners."

The editor of the *Bath Daily Times* wrote: "The disaster of the huge new ship *Titanic* of the White Star Line, reported sinking as the result of a collision with an iceberg off the Grand Banks while on her maiden trip across the Atlantic with 1,200 passengers and a crew of several hundred men, is as extraordinary as it is unexpected. The huge ship was regarded as unsinkable . . . the disaster apparently eclipses everything in maritime annals both in respect [to] the number of lives imperiled in a single ship, and also of the apparent contradiction of the seemingly proved indestructibility of a steel ship built on modern lines."

In announcing the news of the accident, officials of the White Star Line, *Titanic*'s owners, said they remained confident in *Titanic*'s watertight compartments and the fact that other ships, including the *Virginian,* were steaming to her aid.

"A reassuring feature of the accident to the *Titanic* is that a large number of ships appear to be within the big steamer's call. Besides the *Virginian* of the Allan Line, which appears to be the first to have heard of the *Titanic*'s distress, and the White Star Liners *Baltic* and *Olympic,* both of which were reported on the way to the scene, there is also the *Cincinnati* of the Hamburg-American Line, and the Cunarder *Mauritania* . . . ," editorialized one Maine paper.

Although there were no more details available at the time than what the headlines screamed, Mainers knew they would hear the stories sooner than everyone else. This is because it was originally announced the injured liner would be towed to Halifax, Nova Scotia. According to a headline in the *Portland Evening Express and Daily Advertiser* (hereafter known as the *Portland Evening Express*), TITANIC'S PASSENGERS TO GO THROUGH PORTLAND BY TRAINS, Mainers would soon hear the fascinating story firsthand. A special train was being arranged by White Star's J. P. Morgan Jr., son of one of *Titanic*'s owners, and also one of Mount Desert Island's most famous summer residents. The train would stop over in

Portland on its trip back to New York after picking up passengers and crew in neighboring Halifax.

At 11:35 a.m. on Monday, J. P. Morgan Jr. placed a long-distance phone call to Charles Mellen, president of the New York, New Haven & Hartford Railroad Company, ordering this special train to pick up *Titanic*'s passengers and crew. At 12:08 p.m. President Mellen immediately called Mr. McDonald, vice president and general manager of the Maine Central Railroad in Portland, to make arrangements for their arrival. The plan was for the passengers to be taken by the Canadian Pacific Railroad from Halifax to Vanceboro, where they would be brought by the Maine Central Railroad to Portland. In Portland, the train would be under the control of the Boston & Maine.

The railroads involved got their trains under way immediately so that the passengers could be tended to without delay. They planned to have everything ready as soon as the *Carpathia* landed the passengers, making the stops as short as possible to get the large number of passengers and crew to New York as fast as possible. Sixty-one cars were arranged for, including thirty-three Pullmans. *Carpathia* was expected to land in Halifax on Tuesday, and the passengers would be fed in Portland.

The special train left the hub at Boston and carried newspaper reporters and family members of *Titanic* passengers. When the train reached Portland at 7:10 p.m. on Monday night, however, the engineer received news that *Titanic*'s passengers would instead be going directly to New York. In Portland, everyone left the special train and headed back to Boston and New York. As far as anyone knew at this time, all were safe aboard *Titanic*; it was just their destination that had changed.

What the public did not know was that Morgan had arranged accommodations for only 1,400 people—not the 2,100 passengers and crew members that had been on board the *Titanic*.

One early visitor to the White Star Line office in New York on Monday was Vincent Astor, a member of the most socially prominent family among many who visited Bar Harbor each summer. Vincent's father, Colonel John Jacob Astor, and his new step-mother, Madeleine Talmage Force, whom the senior Astor had met in Bar Harbor, were sailing back to the United States aboard *Titanic*. Captain Edward Smith, commander of the newest ship in the White Star fleet, was known as "the millionaires' captain," and Astor was one of that select company. Vincent Astor adored his father; his feelings for his new stepmother, who was younger than him, were not so pleasant.

John Jacob Astor IV was born in Rhinebeck, New York, on July 13, 1864, the son of Mr. and Mrs. William Astor. He graduated from Harvard in 1888 and assumed the management of the family estate, valued at $150 million (about $3.5 billion today) at the time of *Titanic*'s sinking. In 1897 he built the Astoria Hotel, which he later consolidated with the Waldorf Hotel, creating the Waldorf-Astoria. He was also an inventor and author. In 1898, Colonel Astor spent $100,000 of his own money to equip a battery with gunpowder and other equipment during the Spanish-American War, and was made lieutenant colonel. He fought with the Astor battery, landing in Cuba in a hail of gunfire, and later receiving a special commendation for bravery.

For the Astors, cash was just cash; their real currency was social status. Colonel Astor's late mother, always referred to as "*The* Mrs. Astor," coined the term The 400, referring to the top four hundred families in her social circle. The colonel's divorce—which took place a few years before the sinking, during a time when divorce was scandalous—had caused a sensation among that society. In her divorce action, the colonel's first wife, Ava, contended that Astor had had extramarital affairs.

Madeleine Talmage Force, tall, blonde, and a year younger than the colonel's son, Vincent, was from a New York family that had summered in Bar Harbor for years. She met Colonel Astor in Bar Harbor two years before the sinking, in 1910, when she was just seventeen. Astor's family was from Fifth Avenue; Madeleine's was from Brooklyn. In Bar Harbor, Astor's family summered along the fashionable Shore Path; Madeleine's summered closer to Hulls Cove. Though the two island areas were within a few miles of each other, socially, they were miles apart. "The [Force family] had a small cottage in an unfashionable locality, entertained very modestly, and had rather a modest place in fashion's whirl here," wrote the *Bar Harbor Times.*

Madeleine Talmage Force was born on June 19, 1893, the daughter of William H. Force and Katherine Talmage. Her father was active in the shipping and the forwarding business, having been a senior member of William H. Force & Company. He was a director of the Staten Island Rapid Transit Company and the United States Casualty Company. He also served on the New York Board of Trade and Transportation and the New York Chamber of Commerce, among other institutions. His wife, Mrs. Katherine Force, reportedly was grooming her daughters, Madeleine and Katherine, for important marriages.

Madeleine made her name in Bar Harbor playing tennis, winning tournaments there, including many at the Kebo Valley Golf Club. In addition to a golf course, the club also boasted a theater and restaurant, race track, baseball field, and several tennis and croquet lawns.

It is believed that a visit to John Innes Kane by his cousin, Colonel Astor, led to the most shocking romance of its time. Yearly summer visitor John Innes Kane was cousin to John Jacob Astor and grandson of the first John Jacob Astor. Kane was a stockholder of the Country Club of Mount Desert, and Kane's wife was on the Music Committee of the Building of Arts. Kane hired noted architect Fred Savage of Northeast Harbor to design and build a Tudor-style cottage, "The Breakwater," on Bar Harbor's historic

Shore Path in 1904. They had a big black auxiliary yacht, *Idler,* that they kept in Frenchman Bay.

Divorced for only a year, Colonel Astor first saw young Madeleine in 1910 on the tennis courts at the Bar Harbor Swimming Club, where she was a star. A long, two-story building with little windows on the second floor, the front of the club featured tables with umbrellas and chairs, along with a saltwater pool blocked off in the bay, a bathhouse, a reception room, private dressing rooms, and two tennis courts. It later became the Bar Harbor Club.

"To get up from the shore to the street, we had to pass by the wire fence that enclosed the public side of the Swimming Club pool," writes Sylvia Kuson in her book, *My World on an Island.* "That fence was there to keep us apart from the summer colony, whose club it was. Still, it couldn't keep us from looking, and look we did, our eyes round with wonder.

"Around that pool and in it disported the rusticator ladies, dressed to the nines for their afternoon appearances. I remember that I never wondered where the men were—perhaps off on the private golf course—so bemused I was by the ladies," Kuson continues. "As we saw it, they were there to swim, but we were baffled about how they could manage it: every one of them wore, in and out of the water, a wide-brimmed hat, a dress with billowing skirts, long stockings, and, in some cases, gloves that reached from their fingers to their shoulders. Our eyes would travel a circuit of the pool, focus on the swimmers, and see that what we doubted we were seeing was true. They were doing a bogged-down breaststroke."

Though the summer of 1910, the colonel and Madeleine Force were spotted together at various social functions. On September 3, 1910, Colonel Astor, along with his son, Vincent, gave a luncheon at the Swimming Club, following a tennis tournament. Rumors soon began that Astor and Madeleine were involved, the story made more interesting by the difference in their social standing and age. On January 22, 1911, Colonel Astor gave a dinner at the Plaza in New York in honor of Miss Force. Several of her single lady friends and their dates attended.

The following year, the 1911 summer season in Bar Harbor saw record visitors. Cars were still prohibited on Mount Desert Island, so people enjoyed rides in horse-drawn carts. Jesup Memorial Library had just been built. And the hot island gossip was that Colonel Astor and Madeleine Force were to be married.

On August 11, 1911, the rumors were put to rest when Madeleine's father made the official announcement of his daughter's engagement to the colonel. "I called Colonel Astor on the telephone today," Madeleine's father, William Force, said, "and we discussed the matter; it was agreed that I should make the announcement."

Now all gloves were off. The *Bar Harbor Record* reprinted a small editorial from the *Boston Globe:* "The 18-year-old beauty who is to marry Col. John Jacob Astor, now in his 48th year, has the comfort of knowing that only three corespondents were named in the complaint when the colonel was divorced."

On August 20, the *Bar Harbor Record* reprinted a piece from the Philadelphia press:

> For it's off with the old love, and on with the new;
> divorces are easy and we all draw a few.
> The lady is "cute," and she's only eighteen,
> but whether the new Force'll hold him is yet to be seen.

On August 25, the same paper reprinted another piece from the *Boston Globe:* "If Col. Astor's son Vincent is to marry the sister of his father's fiancée [Katherine], he will become his father's brother-in-law, and the complications of relationship in the third generation will be too appalling to predict."

On August 30, the *Bar Harbor Record* printed the following poem, saying "Not dedicated to Col. John Jacob Astor":

Some leaders lead too far ahead,
High-visioned, unafraid;
Yet ages after they are dead
We tread the paths they made.
Some leaders lead too far behind,
Nor seem to keep the track;
Yet they bring on the deaf and blind
Who else would hold us back.
And some seem not to lead at all,
Slow moving on the way;
Yet help the weary feet and small
Of those who else would stray.
Lead on, O Leaders of the Race!
Your work is long and wide;
We need your help in every place—
Before; behind; beside.

Amid the rumors and vicious comments, however, there would be both glamour and adventure for the young Madeleine. The August 12 edition of *Town & Country* magazine featured a large picture of Miss Force from a photograph by Aime Dupont.

A week after the engagement had been announced, on August 19, Madeleine and Colonel Astor took part in the rescue of five shipwrecked men in Newport Sound. They were on Astor's yacht, *Noma,* along with Madeleine's father, proceeding to Newport. Near midnight, the seas were heavy, kicked up by a westerly gale. The yacht's master, Captain Roberts, heard cries of distress. It was the sloop *Zingara,* her sails torn to ribbons by the storm, an upside-down flag serving as a distress signal. Astor, Madeleine, and her father all dressed and hurried to the deck. Crew members from the *Noma* were lowered in a lifeboat, while Madeleine, clad in a heavy polo coat, stood on the deck with her father and Astor.

"Hurry and save the men!" cried Madeleine. When the men were rescued, she said "Beautiful, boys! Nobly done!" She clapped her hands, and was the first to take hold of the ropes as the captain ordered the lifeboat to be hoisted back on deck. She served the men steaming hot coffee and sandwiches. Before leaving the *Noma,* the rescued crew stood up in the cutter and shouted three cheers for Astor, Madeleine, and Mr. Force, as well as Captain Roberts and his crew. "We lost everything, but we do not mind that," said James Mann of the *Zingara.* "We were saved."

At noon on the day after the rescue, the *Noma* steamed away for a two-day ocean-fishing trip for Miss Force's benefit. On board were Astor, Madeleine, her father, and a female companion of Madeleine's. "Miss Force showed much ambition on board this morning, and was without a trace of illness as she walked the decks with Colonel Astor in a white linen yachting suit and wearing a single American Beauty rose, Colonel Astor's favorite flower," said the *New York Times.*

Now that the engagement had been announced, all attention had turned to the ceremony. Astor and Force were silent on the subject. Churches were entering the fray, denouncing the planned nuptials because Astor was divorced. Due to the outrage, the couple had difficulty finding a minister who was willing to perform the ceremony. One minister even refused an offer of $1,000 to do the honors.

On September 8, however, the press reported that it was believed a minister had been found. At the same time, preparations were being made aboard Colonel Astor's yacht, with enough coal loaded on board for a long voyage. At the Force residence in Brooklyn, rush orders were being delivered by dressmakers and milliners. Astor denied rumors that the marriage was imminent, saying the cruise was just a weekend fishing trip. He said the wedding would not take place for at least another three or four days.

The next day, the *Noma,* carrying most of the wedding party, arrived in Newport Harbor at about eight a.m. Vincent rushed to be the first person aboard, but was bested by a deputy sheriff, who served Colonel Astor with lawsuit papers involving the electrocution of a worker at Beechwood, the Astors' summer estate in Newport.

Vincent joined the party for breakfast, after which Colonel Astor captained the motorboat to shore, where he and Madeleine went to city hall to obtain a marriage license. Astor appeared greatly agitated and nervous, but Madeleine was seemingly unconcerned.

The colonel and Madeleine were wed that very day at Beechwood, a great three-story structure. The couple stood in a flower-filled ballroom, their right hands clasped, overlooking the sea. Ironically, storm clouds were gathering. The Saturday ceremony was attended only by members of the immediate families and a few intimate friends. Madeleine was given away by her father, and her sister Katherine was her bridesmaid. Vincent was the best man.

"Miss Force appeared radiant with happiness, and Col. Astor, having recovered from the nervousness which he had exhibited earlier in the day, was calm and self-possessed . . . immediately after the ceremony he gave orders to his chauffeur in a quick, decisive tone," reported one newspaper.

After the ceremony, snacks were served. Accompanied by Madeleine's parents, the newly married couple then took an automobile to the boat landing, where they boarded a launch that took them to the *Noma.* A gentle rain had started to fall. Within fifteen minutes of the ceremony, the Astors were off on their honeymoon, destination unknown to all but the couple.

Just before leaving Beechwood, Colonel Astor gave a statement to the Associated Press: "Now that we are happily married, I do not care how difficult divorce and remarriage laws are made. I sympathize heartily with the most straight-laced people in most of their ideas, but believe remarriage should be made possible, as marriage is the happiest condition for the individual and the community."

The marriage was front-page news in the *Bangor Daily Commercial.* That same day, the *Bangor Daily News* would run an editorial about the marriage: "The outcome means much to the Astors, no doubt. It means more to a Christian civilization that will sanction the purchase of manly and womanly honor with any money price."

A month later, on October 4, the *Bangor Daily News* would run another brief editorial piece: "Now that Colonel Astor is safely—and Pa Force's daughter [is] more or less safely—married, let us turn our attention to getting in the winter's coal."

Two days later, the Newport, Rhode Island, Ministers Union adopted a resolution stating that none of their members should perform a marriage when one of the parties has been divorced. Ministers in Boston would also decry the Astor marriage.

On October 17, 1911, it was announced that the Astors, who had been cruising in southern waters for three weeks, were expected to return to New York at the end of the month, going to their country place at Rhinebeck for a short stay, after which they would open their house on Fifth Avenue, on November 10. They were expected to occupy the Astor box for the first performance at the Metropolitan Opera House on November 13.

According to Joseph H. Choate, an Astor estate lawyer and former ambassador to England, he met Astor at the opera in November. Astor invited Choate to the private box, which held only Madeleine and her sister. "It was an open secret that New York had not looked favorably on the remarriage. The hostility of this dazzling company was evident. Mrs. Astor, scarce out of her teens, faced it with perfect composure. Neither her beauty nor her youth pleaded successfully for her. No friendly glance came their way. I talked with her for five interesting minutes and came away with an impression of intelligence, of charm also, and character."

Choate reported that the Astors planned to entertain on a lavish scale that winter, with dinners, dances, and two grand balls. "But New York declined to be conciliated by these good intentions," said Choate. "It became clear that time must pass before Colonel Astor could expect to find himself surrounded by friends, as of old."

Although considered leaders in society, the Astors had taken little part in any social life since they had returned from their honeymoon. They had scheduled a dinner dance at the New York mansion on January 22, but it was called off. Newspaper reporters in Maine speculated about possible reasons why.

"This question generally asked in the ultra society circles of New York yesterday elected two answers, the first of which was that Mrs. Astor was tired out in maintaining her position as the bride of one of the foremost leaders of society, despite the fact that she is a splendid athlete, her diversion being tennis playing," wrote the *Bar Harbor Record.*

"The second answer was that the charmed circle had not extended the warmest hand of greeting to her. The much-talked-of dance was planned by Col. Astor to launch his bride into the social season, and was one of the first events which the colonel had in mind for her entertainment during the winter. But now he has suddenly cancelled the affair, and come forth with the announcement that on January 26, he and Mrs. Astor will leave on an extended trip up the Nile in his yacht," the report continued. "While the season's round of social gayeties has been under way for several weeks, the Astors have taken but little part in them."

It was presumably for this reason—that the inner circle had snubbed his new bride—that they went abroad to Egypt that winter instead of staying in New York. And it was for this reason that Colonel John Jacob Astor and his wife Madeleine were sailing on the maiden voyage of *Titanic.*

Whether or not she was ready for it, Madeleine Astor was caught up in the whirl of high society.

On Monday, April 15, the true story of the extent of the *Titanic* disaster was already known by some, including a wireless operator in Eastport, Maine, who had listened in as the drama unfolded on the evening of April 14 through the morning of the 15th. The operator worked in a small shack built on the hill near Kendall's Head in 1910, emblazoned with the words UNITED WIRELESS TELE-GRAPH. Its call letters were WQ, and eleven wires ran from the shack. It was ". . . a very freaky station. You can hear it halfway across the ocean," said a Marconi wireless official at the time.

The Eastport wireless operator called the *Frankfurt* and asked about the CQD distress call he had picked up from *Titanic* around midnight. According to Gilbert Balfour of the Marconi Company, Eastport had been interfering with wireless communications between *Titanic* and potential rescue ships all night long.

Reporters from the Associated Press would soon be at the shack, asking for information. For the time being, however, Mainers still believed all was well. When they opened their evening papers, they read headlines like *TITANIC*'S PASSENGERS ARE ALL SAFE / STEAMSHIP BEING TOWED TO HALIFAX, printed in that day's *Portland Evening Express,* followed by the sub-headline, which read: "Have Perilous Experience off Newfoundland Coast." The *Lewiston Evening Journal* that night read ALL PASSENGERS ON *TITANIC* SAVED, followed by: "Removed to Other Steamships which Hastened to Aid of White Star Liner; Damaged Vessel Making Her Way to Halifax under Own Steam."

The *Bath Daily Times* announced *TITANIC*'S PASSENGERS TAKEN OFF SAFELY AND VESSEL STILL AFLOAT, while the evening edition of the *Bangor Daily Commercial* trumpeted: GIANT LINER *TITANIC* RAMS

HUGE ICEBERG. The story recounted how twenty boatloads had already been transferred to *Carpathia,* and that the *Virginian* would reach the site by ten a.m. on Monday morning. This would be eight hours after she sank. Still, their editorial page hinted that all was not good: "A lurking fear remained of possible bad tidings to come."

Vincent Astor had planned to be part of the train that was going through Portland to pick up passengers in Halifax, but his plans changed at the last minute.

William Vincent Astor was born at the Astor mansion on Fifth Avenue on November 15, 1891. He was a delicate child, tall like his father. He had been a sickly baby, and lived an isolated life because of it. At twelve he had appendicitis and had surgery. The boyish-looking Vincent attended Harvard. He had dark eyes and resembled his father, especially the lower part of his face. Vincent was twenty at the time of the *Titanic* disaster, and had been his father's constant companion after the colonel's divorce from his first wife, Ava, in 1909.

After the train was canceled, Astor went directly to the White Star Line offices in New York Monday night, accompanied by A. J. Biddle of Philadelphia, an Astor Trust executive. The halls were crowded with anxious family members and press. By now the names of the surviving *Titanic* passengers aboard *Carpathia* had started to trickle in, alphabetically, starting with First Class. The incomplete list had been posted at the building's entrance, and was well past the As.

Accompanied by Biddle, Vincent spent fifteen minutes with the White Star Line's vice president, Philip Franklin, before leaving the building with tears in his eyes.

II

Can we ever know how those people stood the supreme test? The discipline of the crew. The self-control and obedience of those people so used to command[ing] and [to being] obeyed . . . this unprecedented disaster teaches again the insecurity of our security.

—*Eastern Argus*

The stories coming from the state's newspapers on Tuesday were much bleaker than those that had appeared on Monday.

At 7:15 p.m. on Monday night, the White Star Line announced that the *Titanic* had indeed sunk. They said that the event had occurred at 2:20 a.m., after all her passengers had been transferred to the *Virginian*. Still, not every reporter was convinced that all was well. Reporters noticed that the printed announcement, read by a White Star Line assistant, appeared to be longer than what the assistant read, and mentioned the words "with survivors."

At 8:15 p.m. the White Star Line announced that it was probable a number of lives had been lost, but that no definite number was yet known. This number would not be available, they said, until they knew the exact number of passengers rescued by the

Virginian and the *Parisian,* which would add to the number rescued by *Carpathia.*

At 8:40 p.m. on April 15, Vice President Franklin of the White
Star Line conceded that there had been "a horrible loss of life" in
the *Titanic* disaster. He continued to report that there had been
sufficient lifeboats.

On Tuesday morning, April 16, hope clung briefly that the
Virginian and the *Parisian* had picked up some survivors. At elev-
en o'clock that morning, this hope was dismissed when the *Parisian* reported they had no survivors, as did the *Virginian,* which
said it had "arrived at the scene of the disaster too late to be of
service."

It was the *Portland Evening Express* that announced the bad
news Tuesday morning: PRACTICALLY ALL MEN ON *TITANIC* LOST WITH
SHIP. The paper let readers know the *Carpathia* was due in to port
on Thursday, adding: "[The *Carpathia*] steams slowly to port with
probably only persons who escaped death . . . All hope for details
of the tragedy and its effects are centered on this ship."

Everyone wanted to know what had happened, but details
were few and far between. The papers started publishing the
complete passenger list, and as the only rescue ship, *Carpathia,*
started to wire in the names of survivors, later newspaper editions
also included the partial list of survivors. With a lack of details,
the stark truth of the disaster would come down to a simple com-
parison of the two lists.

JOHN JACOB ASTOR NOT NAMED AMONG THE KNOWN SAVED read the
Portland Evening Express, along with a picture of the millionaire.
Due to misspellings on the survivor list, of which there were
many, it was not immediately believed Madeleine Astor had lived.
It made a certain kind of sense: If Colonel Astor, the richest man
on the ship, could not survive the disaster, what chance had his
wife?

A reporter called Madeleine's father and asked if the rumor that his daughter had perished in the sinking was true. "Oh, my God, don't tell me that!" replied Mr. Force. "Where did you get that report from? It isn't true! It can't be true!"

By 4:30 p.m. on Tuesday, the names of 326 survivors had been received. By the time the paper was published on Tuesday night, all of the names of First Class and some Second Class passengers had been received, totaling 317 of the 700-plus survivors.

The hurried compilation and dissemination of the passenger list caused concern among Maine people. One error was the listing of Richard F. White, who was single, of Brunswick, and his father, Percival Sr. Though they were the only two members of the family traveling on *Titanic,* in the passenger list they were listed as Richard White and his wife, traveling with a maid and manservant. "No word has been heard from Mr. White since the accident to the liner," one newspaper dispatch reported.

Coming from Massachusetts, Richard Frasar White, along with his parents, had returned to his mother's home state of Maine to live when Richard was eighteen, four years before the sinking, as he prepared to attend Bowdoin College. Richard had already spent time in the state, as much of his extended family lived there. He spent summers at a place they simply called "Camp," a large building with a screened-in sleeping porch, located on Mere Point in Brunswick.

Richard's Maine summers were idyllic. Uncle Nungie, an important figure in young Richard's and older brother Percival's life, would teach the boys woodworking. Together they built a miniature town at the camp that they called "Tottle Town." The two brothers and their friend Robert Whittemore would wile away many summer afternoons in a canoe, observing "Loppy Hour." The boys took turns being the beneficiaries: Two would row while the boy in the center of the canoe would relax and read aloud to the two oarsmen.

Richard's parents had difficulties, even though both came from money. Percival Sr., whose ancestors dated back to the *Mayflower,* was born in Massachusetts in 1857. He was fifty-five at the time of the sinking. His grandfather, Joseph White, was a pioneer cotton manufacturer in New England. His father followed in the business, as did Percival and his four brothers.

It was said that wherever Percival Sr. was known, he was loved. Generous to a fault, he was described as representing the fullness and completeness of life. To be in Percival Sr.'s company, with his warm smile and words of welcome, was described as a pleasure. "No better man ever lived than he," said Percival's brother, Zadock Long White. Percival also had two sisters.

Edith White, Richard's mother, looked down on her husband's family, seeing them as flashy. During their courtship, according to their great-granddaughter and family historian, Lucy Sallick, Percival sent Edith a piano as a gift. Edith came from a good Maine family. Her grandparents, Amos and Louisa Warren Wheeler, were from the Brunswick and Topsham area. Her father, William, was also from that area, and had also attended Bowdoin. Her uncle was George A. Wheeler of Castine, a Civil War veteran who, along with his brother, Henry W. Wheeler, wrote a history of Castine and Penobscot, first published in 1875. George had learned Latin and Greek at Bowdoin College and Harvard.

Percival and Edith's son Richard was described as thoughtful, conscientious, filial, faithful, thorough, and eagerly interested in the many-sided world. A man of character and temperament, he was earnest, kind, modest, and efficient.

Percival Jr., Richard's older brother, graduated from Oahu College in Honolulu in 1904, and in 1909, from Harvard, where he received a master's degree in 1910. He became a feature writer for the *Boston Post.*

The Whites had just the two boys, and Richard was always known as "the good son," and Edith's favorite. This may have been due in part to the fact that Richard was an easy baby to care for, while Percival Jr. was more difficult. Despite their differences, the boys were close; in fact, Percival depended on Richard. "Percival was crazy about his brother," said Percival Jr.'s granddaughter, Lucy Sallick.

Richard was interested in nature, and became a registered guide in four counties (Somerset, Franklin, Aroostook, and Piscataquis) for Maine's Inland Fisheries and Game Department, as did his brother. Richard took several canoe trips through the Maine woods, and enjoyed woodworking, making many beautiful and useful things with his hands.

When Richard reached college age, his parents worried about his social awkwardness and whether he would fit in with the family tradition of attending Harvard. They decided on the other family tradition instead—Bowdoin College in Brunswick.

When it came time to move to Maine in preparation for Richard's college career at Bowdoin, the Whites did things in their own unique style. They had originally bought a house that overlooked a graveyard in Edith's native Topsham. According to family lore, after spending just one night there, Edith declared she did not want to wake up every morning to the sight of a graveyard, so the idea of "The Pines" was born. Older brother Percival was commissioned to draw up plans for a new family home, to be located on Brunswick's Maine Street. The Pines eventually became known as a center of hospitality in the town.

True to his nature, Richard took his application to Bowdoin College quite seriously. On May 20, 1908, he wrote to the college's registrar: "As I intend to take examinations in Plane Geometry and Advanced Latin, I should like to know specifically what the requirements in these two studies are," he wrote to the school. Richard had prepared for Bowdoin by studying several languages, including Latin, Greek, and French, as well as algebra and both Roman and Greek history. On Richard's certificate for admission, William Bradbury, principal of the Cambridge Latin School, wrote that Richard "ranks highest of the boys in his class."

As Bowdoin men, Richard's class believed they were charged with the duty to fight for greater equality of opportunity and to give every man his chance, as they had been given theirs. Although they started with 115 students, their class dwindled by 40 between the years of 1908 and 1912.

Along with his classmates in the Class of 1912, whose colors were brown and white, Richard learned the necessities of college life, including the class cheer:

> M-D-C-D-X-I-I!
> Vive la Bowdoin, Rah, Phi Chi!
> Raggedy, Haggedy, Raggedy, Relve!
> Bowdoin, Bowdoin, 1912.

Dick, as he was known around campus, was an active student. From the start he wrote stories for *The Quill*, the school's literary magazine, which was sold both on and off campus. He was elected to the academic fraternity Phi Beta Kappa, and was a member of the athletic Sophomore Squad. In his junior year he would be elected to *The Quill*'s editorial board.

Richard was a prolific writer during his college career. Among other writing projects, in 1909 he penned a poem called "Hawaii's Isle" for *The Quill*, which told of the land his father loved, and where he himself had twice visited.

> Her beauty is like that dark maiden,
> So charming in Wanton Wiles,
> Who were with her barbarous graces
> The Pride of Hawaii's Isle.

In July 1911, *The Quill* published his poem "To a Mockingbird":

Thrive, gentle Hawthorn, thrive
Through thunder doth contrive
To wreck thy form sublime
'gainst ax and gale stand strong
All through the gales long
unscathed by the lapse of time.

Richard's parents' concerns for their son's social awkwardness were well-founded. Although academically successful, he did not always fit in with his Bowdoin classmates. Because of his outside interests, and the fact that his parents and home were just down the road, Richard was not as visible or involved in day-to-day campus life as were his classmates. They complained that the only time he was seen on campus was when he was going from one recitation to another.

"If you ever do see him," wrote the 1912 *Bowdoin Bugle* yearbook staff, before the *Titanic* disaster, "those big spectacles and that pompadour will make you think of the Boston youth who would rather say 'infinitesimal particles of saline humective fluidity' than 'little drops of water.'"

Richard's classmates thought he spent too much time with his head buried in books: "If Dick's strong addiction to study and consequent consumption of great quantities of printed matter have not given him a preference for big words, they have kept him from mingling as much as is best with his fellow students," wrote the *Bowdoin Bugle* staff. Richard would say he was a humble seeker after truth. Replied his classmates: "He should look for it not only between the covers of textbooks and in evil-smelling laboratories, but also in the daily lives and characters of the human beings assembled there."

Richard pursued his academics so earnestly that he finished his college career by the end of February 1912, while his classmates had to finish out the academic year. The additional work would take its toll on young Richard, however; he was described as well-worn by his studies. This gave his father the perfect opportunity to suggest a solution. Percival Sr. made a hobby out of taking maiden voyages on ocean liners. Combining this with his desire to give Richard a restful vacation, along with rewarding him for finishing his studies early, there was only one thing to do: Percival Sr. booked passage for them both on the newest, flashiest ocean liner of them all—*Titanic*.

Richard first traveled with his parents to South Carolina, spending part of the winter there. Then he accompanied his father on a business trip to Europe, departing with Percival Sr. on March 23 on board *Olympic*, *Titanic*'s sister ship. Richard's mother would leave South Carolina to visit Washington, planning to land in New York to greet her husband and beloved son when *Titanic* came into port. They were to have been joined by Percival Jr. Once reunited, the family intended to travel back to Brunswick to prepare for Richard's graduation ceremony. The Whites' housekeeper, Mrs. Anna Coffin, received a letter from Richard in which he outlined their plans for the trip home from Europe aboard *Titanic*.

Richard was on his way home for graduation, a joyous time when his class would celebrate their achievement with speeches before classmates, parents, faculty, and alumni. After the ceremony, they would smoke a peace pipe, cheer the halls of the schools, and march in their caps and gowns from King Chapel onto Maine Street to the Church on the Hill. Several classes were holding their reunions at the time of graduation. There would be dances, fraternity house parties, green lawns and copious shade trees, the bright costumes of the ladies and sharp dress of the gentlemen. Richard and his family would be together for the festivities, and the famous hospitality of The Pines would be in full swing.

When they boarded *Titanic*, this is what graduation meant to Richard and his father, and to his classmates back in Maine. After *Titanic* sank, it would have a much different meaning.

Regardless of the error in the passenger list, Mrs. White could not help but face the fact that their names did not appear on the survivor list. Worried about the fate of her husband and favorite son, Mrs. White cabled Mrs. Coffin from New York, where she awaited the arrival of *Carpathia*, telling their housekeeper, "I will let you know later when I hear definite news."

While no news had been heard about the survival of two members of the White family, much had been reported about the fate of Charles Hays, president of Portland's Grand Trunk Railway.

On Tuesday, the first word received at the Portland railway from the Montreal office was that Charles M. Hays had been saved. Still, uncertainty prevailed; a headline appeared in the Portland papers that day, after the complete list of survivors from First Class had been received, reading PRES. HAYS RESCUED? His name did not appear on the survivor list. By the time of the evening edition, the headline read HAYS PROBABLY NOT RESCUED. The story said there had been no confirmation of the Montreal office's original claim that Hays had indeed been rescued.

Charles Melville Hays of Cushing Island, Maine, was considered one of the most successful American railroad officials of the time. He was born on May 16, 1856, in Illinois, and was in full charge of the Canadian Grand Trunk Railway's American operations. Hays, and the company he was president of, were two of the major influences on the building of Portland's harbor at the turn of the nineteenth century.

Hays was called a genius of far-sighted intelligence. He saw the potential of a railroad that would afford a quick transfer of grain to one of the greatest and most accessible harbors on the North Atlantic, Portland Harbor. Portland provided the resources it saw necessary for shipping, but it was Hays who convinced the city's financial institutions to lend financial aid in order to build two large grain elevators on the waterfront with the capacity of

storing and moving 2.5 million bushels of produce. These elevators, combined with the wharves, afforded facilities for loading
and unloading steamships of the largest capacity, within easy
reach of the ocean.

When it was built by Hays near the end of the nineteenth
century, the facility could handle seven steamships simultaneously; oftentimes 1,400 railroad cars could be seen, waiting to be
unloaded. The station was equipped with a train shed, which shel-
tered an entire train at a time. Business grew at a yearly rate of
100 percent, and by 1912 Grand Trunk Railway was contributing
$2 million per year to Portland as a result of its operations. The
railroad that year was worth $577,356,682.

In 1898 the Portland Board of Trade wrote: "Since the Grand
Trunk [Railway] came under the able management of Charles M.
Hays and his able staff, new life seems to have been imported in
all its departments, especially in the building of a new elevator,
leased by the Grand Trunk [Railway] from the Portland Elevator
Company . . . With the new elevator, tracks, turnouts, engines,
cars, and bridges, we are especially indebted to the Grand Trunk
[Railway] for increasing so largely their facilities at Portland by
extension of the wharves, elevators, and train service, and for so
largely increasing the ocean steamship traffic of this port."

Portland Harbor was known up and down the Atlantic, as well
as in foreign ports, for its quick loading and discharge times. In
fact, the harbor's operations advanced so rapidly that even with
these spacious, modern facilities, the resources were already
taxed soon after they were constructed. Small towns sprouted up
along the Grand Trunk Railway lines in Maine, and factories and
lumber mills were quickly built near them.

The Grand Trunk Railway's terminus was in Portland, and
when it was built, its passenger station—at the time, the largest in
the country—was called by some one of the seven greatest won-
ders of the world. People from everywhere came to Portland just

to see the station, whose granite walls, red-tiled roof, and clock tower were considered a positive addition to the appearance of the city.

Although Charles Hays and his wife Clara spent time in Montreal, they were frequent summer visitors in Maine. The Hays family used to stay at a cottage called the Up and Down House on Ottawa Avenue, located on Cushing Island, off Portland, an exclusive retreat designed by the famous Frederick Law Olmsted. Sometimes they stayed at the Ottawa House, the island's hotel.

Hays had something to look forward to upon his return to the United States from Europe on his *Titanic* voyage. His new home on Cushing Island was due to be completed that year. The house was huge, big enough to sleep twenty people. It was this home where Charles and Clara planned to spend his upcoming retirement. "It was one of the most charmingly located homes on the Maine coast," wrote the *Republican Journal,* "and he felt a pardonable pride in it."

Mrs. Henry Lloyd of Belfast was a dear friend of Hays. It was she who had helped him to get his start in the railroad business, in the passenger department of the Atlantic and Pacific Railroad in St. Louis, where it is believed he met Clara. Hays's hard work helped to move him up in the railroad, until he became general manager of the Wabash Line.

Hays was described as strong of character, very self-possessed, seldom showing anger. He was always at his desk by nine o'clock in the morning, and he set a pace that was difficult for other officials to keep up with. He was fond of a walk before breakfast. Though he served in some other official roles, he never really appealed to popular imagination. He had no interesting little vices, he never lost his head or enthused on a particular topic, and he never tried to shine socially. Though everyone knew him, no one, other than a few intimates, really *knew* him.

It was said that Hays had never even been slightly intoxicated, never gambled, and never swore, except once, saying the word *damn* to a person who had come into his office and tried to blackmail him. Hays's recreational interests were limited; besides his work, he enjoyed trout fishing. He was known by friends as one of the most widely read men they had ever met. He most enjoyed spending time with his family.

Hays was a man of honesty. Early in his railroad career he resigned from a position at the somewhat shady South Pacific Railway, sacrificing a $50,000-a-year salary because he knew that had he stayed, he would have had to sacrifice his principles.

Hays's first step on the ladder of success in the railroad world occurred when the head of the Wabash Line, one of his early employers, came to the office at 6:30 p.m. one evening. A junior clerk, Hays was the only one left in the office.

"Where's the general auditor?" asked the railroad manager, Mr. A. M. Talmadge.

"Gone," replied Hays.

"Where's the chief clerk?"

"Gone."

"Well, where are the other clerks?"

"Gone."

"Gone! Well, *why* are they gone? What's the time?"

"The time?" repeated young Hays. "I don't know." He began to look for a clock.

Talmadge was impressed by Hays's devotion to duty, and the fact that he didn't pay attention to keeping strict work hours. Talmadge learned that Hays had stayed late to complete the very report that Talmadge had come, unexpectedly, in search of.

Charles Hays's family consisted of his wife, Clara Gregg of St. Louis, and their four daughters, Clara, Marjorie, Louise, and Orian, described by those who knew them as beautiful, all adults in 1912. The popular Hays girls had always enjoyed an active social life on Cushing Island, with plenty of men flocking about. It was the difficult pregnancy of one of his married daughters that led to Hays being on board the *Titanic,* in a rush to be by her side. Charles and Clara were accompanied on the ship by his daughter Orian and her husband, stockbroker Thornton Davidson.

With all of the confusion over the names on the survivor list, the lack of details about the sinking coming from the rescue ship, and the incomplete and misleading stories from White Star Line officials, family members were pinning all hope of finding out who was alive or dead on the arrival of the *Carpathia.* With the lack of information coming from that ship, Maine newspapers spent much of Tuesday editorializing.

"The death list will contain an unusual number of prominent names, as many distinguished people had desired to participate in the maiden and [what would be the] final trip of the palatine *Titanic . . .* the people of the world are hushed and saddened today in contemplation of the most terrible marine disaster in the history of civilization, a calamity that brings mourning to homes on both sides of the Atlantic," wrote the *Bangor Daily Commercial.*

"Can we ever know how those people stood the supreme test? The discipline of the crew. The self-control and obedience of those people so used to command[ing] and [to being] obeyed," wrote the *Eastern Argus* of Portland. "This unprecedented disaster teaches again the insecurity of our security."

The *Portland Evening Express* wrote: "What shall we say of the astounding disaster which sent the gigantic new steamship *Titanic* to a grave two miles below the surface of the Atlantic, bearing with her hundreds of precious lives and millions in money? What can we say? What can anybody say that will lessen the shock to the entire civilized world, that will mitigate the mental anguish of the thousands directly affected by the awful catastrophe? . . . That every passenger, that each member of the crew could not have been safely removed, is something that we cannot understand until we hear the real story firsthand from the survivors."

III

The uncertainty which for three days has been surrounding the fate of the passengers on the doomed steamer, in view of all circumstances, has been the very refinement of torture.
—*Portland Evening Express*

Life in Portland and the surrounding area had nearly come to a halt. According to the *Portland Evening Express's* April 19 edition: "Portland as well as larger cities feels the effect of the terrible calamity which has befallen so many well-known people, and all social affairs were at a standstill today, for there were few which had the courage to send out invitations in the face of the world's sorrow."

Everything seemed to stop except the clicking of the wireless, bringing the names of the survivors to shore. Even that noise was cut off Wednesday morning due to a violent electrical storm in the Atlantic, which the *Carpathia* had to endure.

Once wireless contact had been reestablished, the list of survivors from First and Second Class was continued. When the names of Third Class survivors started coming through, it was considered confirmation that the complete list of First and Second Class survivors was now complete. *Carpathia* reported "that [the] list of first- and second-class passengers and crew sent to shore. *Chester* will relay list third-class passengers when convenient to *Carpathia.*"

All along the East Coast amateur radio operators jammed the airwaves, straining their ears for news. Finally, the *Carpathia* sent the names of some Third Class passengers to Portland via the *Chester,* a US Navy scout cruiser, which relayed the names to the *Salem,* and then on to the naval station at Newport, Rhode Island, for official use. This list, secured under great difficulty, was also received by a wireless operator in Portland and transmitted throughout the country and overseas. Many of the names were foreign and difficult to translate, but eventually, 118 names were transmitted.

"Portland was a prominent place in the news-gathering work throughout the night as the first list of third-class passengers taken from the *Titanic* by the *Carpathia* [was] received by wireless here. [The] list was flash-broadcast throughout the country and even to England before the list had been completed in other parts of the country," wrote the *Portland Evening Express.*

The revenue cutter *Androscoggin,* captained by George M. Daniels and anchored in Portland, was made ready to assist the *Chester* if need be. Her bunkers were filled with coal and provisions were loaded for an extended trip. Navy officials in Washington, D.C., wired her to ask when she could depart. Captain Daniels replied that he could leave port at a moment's notice. She was not called into service.

The *Lewiston Evening Journal* ran a cartoon on its front page, featuring Uncle Sam standing alone on a pier while the *Carpathia* is seen in the distance, steaming to port.

The *Portland Evening Express* showed a diagram of the ship superimposed on a map of downtown Portland. The ship extended from Preble to Oak Streets. It was wider than Congress Street.

"The tragic loss of the ill-fated steamer *Titanic* was the sole topic of conversation in shipping circles yesterday," wrote the daily *Eastern Argus.* The general consensus among those talking about the disaster was that the ship must have received a terrible blow from the iceberg, which must have stabbed all her parts and disabled her watertight bulkhead connectors.

Officers of the SS *Scotian,* docked in Portland, shared a similar opinion: "I believe that the *Titanic* had her broadside torn open, and in such an event there was not the slightest chance to save her, as the bulkheads and compartments would then be of no help," said one unidentified officer of the *Scotian* to the *Portland Evening Express.* "The fact that she remained afloat only a short time seems to me good evidence that the side of the liner was torn open by the ice."Another train of thought was that the ship must have hit the iceberg head-on, the great weight of the ship causing the ocean liner to buckle amidships, busting the watertight compartments.

Captain David Dow, veteran skipper of the *Carmania,* spoke with a little more authority. He had just arrived in Portland on Saturday, the day before the *Titanic* struck the iceberg, and had maneuvered through the same ice field.

Dow gave a description of all the steps a captain would have to go through: closing the watertight doors, ordering the lifeboats prepared, issuing a distress call. He was asked what happens in general aboard a ship that finds itself in a situation such as *Titanic's.* Dow responded that there was probably a lack of panic, as the majority of passengers were Anglo-Saxons or of the Northern races of Europe, "which are as a whole inclined to reasonable coolness in moments of stress," the *Bangor Daily Commercial* reported. Dow added that the officers and crew would have prevented any panic from interfering with reasonable work.

Dow was asked what steps would be taken if the men panicked and tried to rush the boats at the expense of the women and children. "Club 'em back," Dow replied.

F. J. Illsley of Portland, one of the leading civil engineers of the time, said the ship, in its final resting place, would not be crushed by the great pressures of the depth of water she was in. He opined that she would stay practically intact for eighteen or twenty years, but that after that time, the steel would corrode and loosen, eventually falling apart. He said he believed no one would ever reach the *Titanic* because of her depth.

Commander Robert Peary, director of the recent North Pole expedition, a Bowdoin man, and a friend of Colonel Astor's, was in the city for the Bowdoin reunion. He told the *Bath Daily Times* he could not understand how the *Titanic* accident had happened on such calm seas.

"The story of the terrible disaster of the steamship *Titanic* on Sunday night, off Cape Race, has given many a Maine heart a severe wrench and caused grief, which the years had supposed to have buried, to spring up anew," wrote one newspaper.

The loss of the *Portland* in 1898, fourteen years earlier, with its scores of Maine men, women, and children headed from Boston to Portland, was a frequent topic. That ship had left port in a bad storm and was last heard from on Saturday night, November 26, when personnel at the Highland Light lifesaving station heard distress whistles from a steamer believed to be the *Portland.* In the days that followed, many bodies of the 150 people on board washed ashore at various points along the Massachusetts coast, and wreckage had continued to wash ashore since then from time to time.

Mrs. David A. Calhorn of Mountain View Park, Portland, reminisced about her voyage eight months before aboard the *Columbia.* This ship had struck an iceberg head-on off the Grand Banks near Cape Race on August 11, 1911, at 7:15 p.m., during a thick fog. The watertight compartments of that ship, and the fact that she was not going full speed, were credited for her not sinking.

John E. Warren of Westbrook remembered the huge loss of life aboard the *Sultana* in 1865. It was during the Civil War, and the steamer had taken on board 1,900 paroled Union soldiers at Vicksburg. A boiler had burst as the ship made its way up the mighty Mississippi, and roughly 1,300 men died. Mr. Warren had witnessed some of the rescues.

The most coincidental shipping incident that was remembered, however, occurred in the fall of 1900 off Hampden. A British tramp steamer from Glasgow, Scotland, was headed to Bangor to load lumber. She had survived a hurricane during her voyage, and as she approached Bangor, she found her nose stuck in the mud off Hampden. When the high tide finally floated her free later in the day, she overshot her berth at High Head and had to be warped back to the Maine Central wharf.

"Yes, we had a rough passage, but no worse than is to be expected at this time of year," said the ship's captain, William Dawson.

The tramp steamer's name was *Titanic*.

The subject of safety aboard ships was another popular topic of conversation. The *Portland Evening Express* published this article soon after the disaster:

> Owners of motor boats right here in Casco Bay may, if they choose, find a moral in the tragedy of the *Titanic*. A thousand times the great ship might have crossed the broad Atlantic with never a mishap, then upon the thousand and first passage, as happened to be the case upon her maiden voyage, she proved wickedly wanting in what should have been the foremost consideration of her designers and owners—proper life-saving equipment.
>
> Right here at the beginning of the season let the motor boatman be sure that he has the proper equipment as required

by law. And let him not only satisfy the law, but also his own conscience in the matter. A pail of dry sand covers the requirements as to a fire extinguisher, but every boatman knows that sand soon becomes damp, and in case of necessity could not be thrown so as to spread and smother a blaze. Why not obtain, then, one of the extinguishers of proven efficiency, which will throw a liquid that immediately turns to a fire-smothering gas into any out-of-the-way nook or corner of the boat? The first cost may be more than the pail of sand, but if it should be needed, you will never regret the outlay.

The people of Bath remembered the idea of their neighbor, the late Charles D. Hooker, to have large steamers equipped with a large, detachable deck house. He later changed that idea to having a steel case strapped to the deck, large enough to hold everyone aboard. Hooker made a model of the case, which would have air tanks to provide oxygen to passengers and to keep it afloat. The case was small at the bottom so that it would remain upright after launching, and had upright pipes for signaling. The model would burn later in a mill fire.

"Had such an arrangement, or several of them, been on the *Titanic,* countless lives would have been spared," wrote the *Bath Daily Tribune.*

Willmore Portell of Chester talked about a life preserver he had spent seven years working on, which he offered to demonstrate. He said he had tested the four- or five-pound life preserver in the ocean with a dummy weighing three hundred pounds. Of course, Portell's device did not take into account the freezing temperature of the water *Titanic* sank in.

The state's newspapers also took the White Star Line to task for its initial misleading news about the safety of *Titanic* after she hit the iceberg. "That so many New England residents were on board the ill-fated *Titanic* brings home to this section that terrible tragedy of the sea," wrote the *Eastern Argus* of Portland. "Some explanation is properly demanded why the news of the loss of the

Titanic was withheld from the public for more than twenty-four hours. There is no reason to doubt that the main facts of the disaster must have been known in some quarters a few hours after it occurred. Throughout Monday, the newspapers throughout the world were publishing reassuring bulletins with a wealth of fake details, the product of a vivid imagination. The families and friends of those on board were lulled into a belief that all was well, and the general public was led to indulge rose hopes that so far as passengers and crew were concerned, everything was all right. When the truth was known at last, it came with all the more crushing force . . ."

While Mainers were talking about the disaster, some feared that loved ones and acquaintances might be on board. Miss Ethel Crockett, prominent in Rockland society before her marriage to Mr. Ross I. Barton, had been touring France and England with her husband. The Bartons had hoped to sail on *Titanic,* but found there were no staterooms left to their liking. Instead, they sailed aboard the *Cymric,* which left Liverpool the same day *Titanic* left Southampton. They arrived in Portland safely, two days after *Titanic* sank.

Bangor residents were worried about Mark Geghigan, a young man who worked as a chauffeur for a few Bangor families. He had traveled to Ireland to visit family members and was expected to return on the *Titanic,* to begin work for Bangor resident Charles A. Gibson. Geghigan was known to be prompt with his engagements, and nothing had been heard from him since *Titanic* had sunk. "If he does not reach Bangor within the next few days, grave fears of his safety will be entertained," wrote the *Bangor Daily News.* Fortunately, Geghigan was not aboard the *Titanic.*

People in Bath thought they had lost Joseph Marroni, proprietor of the Kennebec Fruit Company. Marroni had sent a letter to Frank Feurri, manager of the fruit company store in Bath, stating he would sail home from England early after Easter, but did not name the ship he planned to take, as was common at the time. It was later learned he was not aboard *Titanic.*

Weston Lewis and family of Gardiner were feared to be aboard the ill-fated ship on their return from Europe, but were later found to have returned on a German liner.

Hugh Chisholm Jr., twenty-six, had his dying father, a Maine timber leader, to credit for his not sailing on *Titanic.* The senior Chisholm was a founder of the Oxford Paper Company, the Otis Falls Paper Company in Livermore Falls, and the International Paper Company. The junior Chisholm had booked passage on *Titanic,* but shortly after doing so received a cable advising him of his father's serious illness. Chisholm was anxious to get home to be with his father, and so took another liner and arrived earlier, and safely. The senior Chisholm died three months later at the age of sixty-six.

The name *Baxter* appeared on the passenger list, and friends and family in Portland were concerned that it might refer to James P. Baxter and family, of that city. After many inquiries, they discovered on Tuesday that it was a different Baxter.

The Debe family of Skowhegan entertained fear for Pete Debe of that city. Debe had traveled to Italy in January to collect his niece, Miss Virginia Debe, after her father had been killed in that country. It turned out that they were also not aboard the doomed ship.

Members of the Abyssinian Church of Portland were disturbed when Reverend Clifford Miller had not returned from a three-month trip abroad. The *Portland Evening Express* described Reverend Miller as being in high standing with his congregation, having won many friends during his time in Portland. He was engaged to be married that summer to a lady from South Carolina who was also worried he might be a *Titanic* passenger. His exact travel plans back to Maine were not known, except that he planned to arrive around April 21. He had not been heard from in some time.

It would turn out that Reverend Miller was aboard the *Niagra.* He arrived in Portland on Tuesday, April 17, two days after the sinking. Though he was spared the fate of those aboard *Titanic,* his ship nonetheless had faced a challenging trip through the same icebergs and ice floes. He rested in New York for three days before continuing on to Maine.

Unfortunately, several people in Maine *did* have relatives aboard the *Titanic.*

Reverend John Butler, formerly of Jackman—who had been preaching at the congregational church in East Sumner for five months before the sinking—had a brother on board. Reginald Fenton Butler was twenty-five and traveling in Second Class. He was engaged in real estate business and was on his way back to America. He was lost in the sinking. Reverend Butler tendered his resignation from the church a month after *Titanic* sank.

Mrs. Cyrus C. Babb of Augusta had a brother, Howard B. Case, formerly of Baltimore, aboard *Titanic.* He was living in London, where he made his home, and was manager of the Vacuum Oil Company. Case's name was not on the survivor list that was transmitted to shore, but he was reported as rescued. He actually went to his death on *Titanic,* helping to fill lifeboats. He was last seen on deck by Mrs. William T. Graham, calmly lighting a cigarette and waving good-bye. He was mistakenly sent a telegram aboard *Carpathia,* which read "Heartiest congratulations."

Edwin Kimball Sr. of Paris, Maine, was concerned about his son, Edward Nelson Kimball. The junior Kimball, who was forty-two at the time of the sinking, was traveling with his wife, Gertrude. Edward and Gertrude both resided in Boston, where the junior Kimball was the president of the Hallett, Davis Piano Company of Boston. Relatives of Kimball's called from Maine to ask a friend to check with the Boston office of the White Star

Line on the status of Edward and Gertrude. The survivor list had erroneously listed Mr. and Mrs. Edwin Kimberly. The Kimballs were rescued from *Titanic* in Lifeboat 5.

Andrew Latimer, fifty-five, *Titanic*'s chief steward, was well-known in Portland. He had served as chief steward aboard the ship *Labrador* of the Dominion Line. The last person from Maine to see Latimer alive was Mrs. Richard McNabb of Spring Street in Portland. They ate together at the Royal Avenue Hotel, one of the most popular hostelries in Belfast, Ireland, the night before *Titanic* sailed. Joining them were *Titanic*'s First Class second steward George C. Dodd, forty-four, who had formerly served as butler to J. Bruce Ismay, the White Star Line managing director, and Edward Parsons, thirty-five, *Titanic*'s chief storekeeper. Mrs. McNabb was visiting friends in Belfast when she ran into Latimer. Latimer and Dodd attempted to persuade Mrs. McNabb to join them on the voyage, and she was almost convinced, but at the last minute she chose to sail on the *Laurentic.* All three crewmen died in the sinking. "Andy Latimer has gone to his death with hundreds of others and will never be seen more upon our streets," said the *Portland Evening Express.*

Alfred Verquesse of North Vassalboro, a worker at a woolen mill, thought he saw his brother's name on the passenger list. Victor Verquesse was a former resident of North Vassalboro, but had spent the last few years in Philadelphia. Victor had left Philadelphia about a month before the sinking to sell the family estate in Tournai, Belgium. Alfred had heard nothing from his brother since he had left to take care of that business. Traveling from Belgium to Ohio, Mr. Victor Verquesse went down with the ship, his body never recovered. It is lost to history whether or not this was Alfred Verquesse's brother or not.

Frank Millett, second cousin and dear friend of Dr. Adelbert Millett of Belfast, was also a passenger. Frank Millett was born in New Bedford, Connecticut, in 1846. He served as a drummer boy in the Civil War, and at its completion entered Harvard, graduating in 1869. He became a newspaper reporter, covering the Russian-Turkish War. Millett was distinguished in his field, but gave it up to become an artist. He had completed four panels for the Supreme Court room of the then-new Wisconsin state capitol. He had also finished paintings of New Bedford's whaling industry, which were to accompany him on the voyage.

Millett was lost in the sinking. His body was recovered, clad in evening dress—black pants, a gray jacket, and a light overcoat.

Aboard *Titanic*, from a letter mailed at a stop at Queenstown, Scotland, Millett wrote a letter to a friend: "Queer lot of people on the ship. There are a number of obnoxious, ostentatious American women, the scourge of any place they infest, and worse on shipboard than anywhere."

The sinking of the *Titanic* seemed to bring out the poet in several Maine people. The *Daily Kennebec Journal* ran a poem by Elizabeth Merrill:

"The Two Giants"

Proudly from old England
Sailed the great ship away,
Cheers rang on the cool air
As it passed down the bay.
Dark was it and mighty
Ribbed with iron and steel
Built to conquer nature—
Perfect from tower to keel.
Out of the weird northland
Came a giant all in white,
No man saw this giant—
It came at dead of night.
Down through seething waters
To those so still and calm,
Sailing to the southward

Where grow the rose and palm.
Night was cool and starlit,
Each giant held its way,
One was dark and somber
While one was veiled with gray;
One was built by labor,
And one was built by God.
Both on a maiden journey
O'er highway never trod.
Slow moved the white giant
Upon the changing tide—
Fast sailed the black giant
Like bridegroom seeking bride.
Calmly the white giant
Tore open the black breast
Then swept on to southland
To find its long-sought rest.
Stars of night were gazing
At giants of a day—
One to sink in ocean,
And one to melt away.
Parted loved and loving,
On earth no more to meet—
Some have made the harbor,
Some sleep at the sea's feet.
Tears must fall for lost ones,
And tears for those that stay;
Life for life was given,
As the ship sank away;
Great souls softly singing
"Nearer My God to Thee,"
Dead—they live forever—
Thought lost—far out at sea.

The *Lewiston Daily Sun* published a short poem by Jane Marsden of that city:

"The *Titanic*"

Down in her grave is the Queen of the Seas,
Heroes unnumbered have gone with thee,
Nations are mourning for thee today,
All the wide world is in sympathy.
Nearer, oh, nearer, my God, to Thee,
Rang o'er the waves of the cruel blue sea.
Heroes, and heroines, staunch and brave,
Sank to their rest in a watery grave.
Nearer to God of their souls are they,
Sleeping in peace until Judgment Day,
Leaving this world here a lesson for all,
Nearer, my God, at duty's call.

The *Eastern Argus* ran a poem about the sinking of the *Portland:*

'Twas a terrible tale that we heard from the sea,
And it brought its unspeakable woe,
For it told of the dead ones who nevermore
The light of their presence could know
That the *Portland* had sunk 'neath the turbulent wave,
And all who had sailed found a watery grave.

"The *Titanic* tragedy was bad enough itself, without having to read some of the so-called poetry being written about it," wrote the *Portland Evening Express.*

In New York at the Astor offices, Vincent Astor, holding out hope for his father and stepmother, was in almost constant communication with White Star, the press associations, and newspaper offices, taking breaks only to eat brief meals at his mansion.

On Wednesday the *Carpathia* had answered a specific inquiry as to whether or not Colonel Astor was on board: The rescue ship confirmed that while Mrs. Astor had survived, Vincent's father had not.

Vincent reached the end of his physical endurance on Wednesday, collapsing at the Astor offices. He was taken home where, in time, he recovered.

IV

It was a long, hard night which started then.
—Lewiston Evening Journal

Early on the morning of April 18, *Carpathia* was believed to be off Nantucket at about six a.m., passing the Nantucket Lightship, the first American beacon the survivors would see on their trip home. They had 192 more miles to go before they would arrive in New York. The arrival at the lightship also coincided with a cold nor'easter, which provided the rescue ship and her devastated passengers with some of the heaviest seas they would encounter on their return home. The storm was said to have sped up their journey by a fraction of a knot. The passengers expected to see their first sight of land by afternoon.

By now the public was craving information. The *Carpathia* was still busy broadcasting the survivor list, and when that was completed, the two wireless operators—one of whom was the sole surviving *Titanic* wireless man—turned their attention to personal messages, which were paid for. One wireless read: "I am praying that my husband has been picked up by another steamer." There was no time to wire any details of the sinking. The world would just have to wait one more agonizing day for *Carpathia*'s arrival, expected the next day, Friday, April 19.

"The world is being held in needless suspense, apparently, by the mistaken policy being pursued by the steamboat officials concerned in the terrible *Titanic* disaster," wrote the *Portland Evening Express.* "What explanation can be given for the silence of the *Carpathia?* . . . In the meantime the public mind is being harrowed beyond all necessity with speculation and guesswork, which ought long ago to have been set at rest."

Stephen Griffin and Horace Perry, two young men from Portland, were listening in to *Carpathia*'s transmissions. They had made a wireless outfit to demonstrate at the Walker Manual Training School, building their equipment at the school, where they were considered the best in their training section. They picked up commercial messages from the *Carpathia*, most of which were simple transmissions, like AM SAFE, signed by the sender. The dedicated amateurs kept the messages private.

In the Thursday edition of the *Lewiston Evening Journal,* a columnist named "Madame Myself," who was described as a "well-known Lewiston woman who wrote many good things for one of Maine's newspapers," wrote of the disaster: "It is hard to conceive of the entire population of a town of the size of Falmouth or Freeport, for instance, being herded together in a single ship and within the space between darkness and daylight of another morning, simply disappearing from the face of the world, never to be seen again."

A committee of thirteen of the most prominent women in New York society was formed with the purpose of taking care of the surviving steerage passengers, and eagerly awaited *Carpathia*'s arrival. Mrs. Louisa Satterlee, daughter of J. P. Morgan, was on the committee. Morgan, a prominent member of the Mount Desert Island summer colony—and one of *Titanic*'s owners—was watching the unfolding tragedy with great interest. Morgan had attended the launching of the *Titanic* in Belfast, Ireland, on May 31, 1911, considered an event of international importance.

John Pierpont Morgan's first real introduction to Mount Desert Island was in 1875, when he and his wife, Fanny, took a steamer to Portland. The party consisted of Mr. and Mrs. Morgan and two of her sisters. They arrived in Portland and continued to sail along the coast, arriving in Bar Harbor and staying at the Rodick House, a popular hotel, on a Saturday. On Sunday they attended church. They spent Monday driving around the neighborhood of Northeast Harbor. Morgan arranged a grand picnic for Tuesday at Great Head and Sand Beach with friends and other guests at the Rodick House. The trip was especially meaningful to Mrs. Morgan, who had spent time on the island with her own family as a girl.

"Her girlish impressions of the beauty of Mount Desert Island were revived and intensified," wrote her son-in-law, Herbert Satterlee. "Moreover, she now had the delight of showing her favorite places to Pierpont, just as he had acted as her guide in England and on the Continent, and he shared her enthusiasm for the island." The Morgans spent another ten days on the island, going on excursions and picnics. Mr. Morgan spent one rainy day playing cards. "It was a real vacation," said Satterlee.

The Morgans were early summer people of Bar Harbor, before the location became fashionable. They were drawn there by the water, where Morgan often sailed his private yacht, the *Corsair.* When the *Corsair* came into Bar Harbor's Frenchman Bay, local rowboats went around in circles to show respect. Leading summer colonists would be invited aboard, and there were many parties, both on board and ashore.

In 1897 Morgan raced *Corsair* in a yacht race, sponsored by the New York Yacht Club, which, for the first time, was extended all the way to Bar Harbor. At the end of the competition, the fleet anchored in Northeast Harbor. The next day they cruised around to Bar Harbor, where Morgan had arranged a barge-load of fire-works. The race was considered a success.

Morgan was no novice on the water. In 1899 Mrs. Morgan sailed home aboard the *Oceanic,* one of the largest vessels of her kind at the time. After the health officer cleared the boat, Morgan's *Corsair* came alongside.

Herbert Satterlee recalled the event:

> Word ran around the decks of *Oceanic* that Mr. Morgan was coming on board, and necks were craned over rails and heads came out of portholes to see him. As the tide swirled around the bottom of both vessels, Mr. Morgan, cigar in mouth, grasped the lower end of the rope ladder the doctor had just climbed down on. Swinging from the ladder, Morgan fixed his straw hat more firmly on his head as his launch left. He was sixty years old, weighed 210 pounds, and [had] never exercised regularly in his life.
>
> As everyone watched, he scaled the height of a four-story house. Some passengers placed bets on his chances. When his face, dripping with perspiration, appeared over the rail, he got where he could throw his leg over it, he waved aside all out-stretched hands, and asked, "Where is Mrs. Morgan?," and without pausing, followed the steward down to her cabin.

In 1901, while anchored off Bar Harbor, Morgan received the news via cable that one of his grandchildren had been born.

In 1911, Morgan purchased property at Great Head on Mount Desert Island for his daughter, Mrs. Louisa Satterlee. He went to Egypt in January of 1911, sailing on the *Olympic.* To round out the year, Morgan would attend a coronation in London. "J. Pierpont Morgan was the only commoner who had a seat among the peers at the coronation," read a cable from London. "What is your own idea of J. Pierpont Morgan as a commoner?" asked the *Bangor Daily News.*

Morgan had booked passage home in 1912 aboard *Titanic*, but at the last minute had decided to lengthen his European vacation, canceling his plans.

White Star Line vice president Philip Franklin was asked about a rumor that Morgan had called the White Star office on Monday, the day of the sinking, demanding that the extent of the disaster be suppressed until after the stock market had closed. Franklin emphatically stated that neither he nor Morgan had known the ship had sunk until Monday night.

In light of the sinking, Mrs. J. P. Morgan Jr. canceled the coming-out party for her daughter, Jane Morgan, in New York. Satterlee described J. P. Morgan as entirely absorbed by the news. Many of his friends were on board, and the captain and ship's officers were all old shipmates of his. He was also deeply hurt by news reports that his company had put money ahead of safety.

By Thursday, it seemed that the survivor list was complete, and had been fully transmitted. If a name was on the list, it brought comfort to a family. If it was not, it brought sorrow.

Sorrow was the case for the Kirkland family of Maine.

On Thursday, the *Portland Evening Express* would print the story that a Bangor man, Reverend Charles L. Kirkland, was believed to be on board *Titanic*. The name "Reverend C. L. Kirkland" (as their father signed his name) on the Second Class passenger list, but not on the survivor list, caused fear for Kirkland's six adult children, Henry, Myrtle, Allen, Algie, Alma, and Maud. "There is a possible chance of it being another Mr. Kirkland," the *Old Town Enterprise* wrote, holding out hope.

Born in 1841, Charles Leonard Kirkland started out life in New Brunswick, the son of a cabinetmaker and a housewife. Life was hard and sorrowful for Kirkland, his mother dying when he was just seventeen. In 1864 he married Rachael Peters Warman, a fellow Baptist, in Kent County, Canada. Son Henry was born in 1868 in Canada, and was brought to Maine by Charles and Rachael in 1869. Their next child, Myrtle, would be born in New Brunswick in 1870, and son Allen was born on Deer Isle. They later had twins, Grace and George, and the baby of the family, Pearl.

In 1876 Reverend Kirkland—who was Baptist, but was comfortable preaching for other denominations, as well—would ply his trade at the Methodist Church in North Brooksville. A year later, in 1877, the Kirklands would arrive in Chester. This was a turning point for the Chester Baptist Church. Reverend Kirkland's preaching was called earnest and pervasive, and manifested a new interest in the things of God. People started to attend services, interested in salvation.

In 1887, an extension of the Canadian Pacific Railroad was built through the back part of Chester, Maine. This railroad brought new church members from as near as Aroostook and as far away as Prince Edward Island. Church services were held at the town hall in Winn Village, and a series of evangelistic meetings was held at the Snow School House in South Winn. The new congregants were said to be a great help when it came to singing. Many people were "saved" as a result of these meetings; on Sunday, May 15, 1887, Kirkland used the Penobscot River to baptize ten of his congregation, including an eighty-five-year-old woman named Mrs. Chamberlain.

With the reverend's professional triumph came great personal tragedy. In 1888, three of Kirkland's children—the twins, twelve-year-old Grace and George, and two-year-old Pearl, the baby of the family—all died.

In 1889, at the quarterly meeting of the Chester Free-Will Baptist Church, Kirkland was awarded the post of minister of the gospel by Elder Horace Graves, "to share in the joys and sorrows." He served there until 1890.

Three years later, in 1892, Reverend Kirkland arrived in Parkman. He preached twice in May, and on July 10 began to preach three-fourths of the time for a year. During the 1890s the meeting house was shared by Methodist, Baptist, and Adventist congregations, and all denominations united in supporting him. Reverend Kirkland continued preaching there through 1894. During this time Reverend Kirkland had the honor of performing the wedding service of his daughter Maud to Nathan Elden, a local farmer.

In 1895 Reverend Kirkland moved on to Danforth, preaching for the Baptist Church congregation at the Danforth church, for the first time on February 17. The congregation would send for him again, and he preached on March 10 and 17. On March 19 the church decided to hire Kirkland for the coming year at the rate of $300 per year, along with use of the parsonage. A letter from the church at Athens, where Reverend Kirkland had also preached, helped sway the vote. On March 24, fifteen members of the church met and voted him in as a member of the church. Kirkland would complete his duty to the Danforth Baptist Church in August of that year.

The following year, 1896, was another tough year personally for Reverend Kirkland. His wife, Rachael, mother to his nine children, died of septicemia, caused by a traumatic event, the details of which are not known. Also that year his two-month-old grandson Pearly Elden would die of cholera.

Two years later, in 1898, he would marry Nellie Carvell of Danforth. The Baptist minister and the divorced Carvell would be joined in marriage by a justice of the peace. Four years later would be another rough one: Grandchildren Ruth and Alonzo Elden died—Ruth of cholera, and Alonzo of acute enteritis.

Reverend Kirkland would later move on to Bangor. His last known residence was 2 Howard Street, at a boardinghouse.

Whether Nellie was with him or not is unknown. He had no particular charge of a church at the time.

In 1912 he traveled to Saskatchewan, Canada, to visit a sister. In April, back in Maine, Kirkland's family, including his son Henry, who worked at Old Town Canoe, knew it would soon be time for him to return to Maine, but did not know exactly when or on which ship he would sail. As Reverend Kirkland boarded *Titanic* in Glasgow, his family had no idea that he was traveling on that particular ship. It was not until the papers printed the passenger list that the Kirkland children became concerned.

As Thursday came to a close, Mainers were still under the impression that the *Carpathia* would not be in until Friday, and that they had another day of torturous waiting to endure. They were given relief, however, when at 3:15 p.m. the White Star Line advised the public that *Carpathia* was actually due to arrive on Thursday night, not Friday morning as had been expected.

As the hours ticked by on Thursday, the arrival time continued to shift. Whereas originally the ship was due in by one a.m. on Friday, it soon changed to eleven p.m. on Thursday—then ten p.m., then nine p.m.

"Notwithstanding the fact that tomorrow is Patriot's Day, the regular editions of the *Express-Advertiser* will be printed because of the widespread desire to know the facts in relation to the wreck of the steamship *Titanic*," wrote the Portland paper.

With the change in arrival date, the state's daily newspapers swung into action. A special edition of the *Lewiston Evening Journal* was ordered. After the news of the Thursday landing was released, the phone lines lit up for several minutes. Editors and writers were ordered for immediate duty. Compositors and linotype operators and others in the composing room were told to report at four o'clock Friday morning, and others at six. Everyone would show up early, excited, with cheery greetings and big smiles.

On Thursday afternoon the circulation manager was notified about the special edition, and he immediately got in touch with all of his carriers. The delivery boys were gathered together by messenger and telephone, but three were missing. A message was sent to the Empire Theater on the chance that they might be there. "The message was flashed upon the screen by the stereopticon, and five minutes later, three excited lads were on the job in the *Journal* circulation room."

The first of the linotype operators to come in was an employee named Anna. Water dripped from her umbrella from the Thursday evening rain, and a good-natured smile covered her face as she put the first leads up. Her arrival was followed by a constant stream of other employees reporting for duty. "Girls and men came in laughing and joking about having to work on a morning paper, and then went to work to clean the copy which was piled up high. It looked as though they were buried, but the story was interesting, the takes were long, and the entire crew, determined."

Before eight p.m., part of the staff of editors and writers were in the office, preparing background stories and laying out plans for the night. At 8:45 p.m. a telegraph operator for the paper, P. J. "Patsy" O'Conner, came in to work, hung up his coat, and sat at his machine. He started translating the clicking signals coming in over the news wire, using the typewriter in front of him to record the transcribed information.

The first news to come in, Patsy simply translated verbally: "Captain . . . Smith . . . shot . . . himself . . . just . . . before . . . the . . . ship . . . went . . . down!"

"Crazy," said the telegraph editor.

"It was a long, hard night which started then," wrote the *Lewiston Evening Journal.*

The wire started churning out information rapidly at this point. Just after seven p.m., the managing editor of the *Lewiston Evening Journal* received word from W. C. Jefferds, the Maine agent for the Associated Press, that *Carpathia* was about to dock. Soon an order came from the AP across the wire: "On the arrival tonight of the *Carpathia,* all available matters will be sent E.O.S. [extraordinary service], and therefore, for immediate publication in both morning and evening papers." This order meant that the deadline times for stories issued by the AP to be used in special editions had been lifted.

Later still, the details of the disaster so eagerly awaited were starting to come through the wire, which, for the last four days, had sent only names.

"It told the waiting editors and reporters that the greatest news story since the firing upon Fort Sumter would soon be ticking off that same little sounder, and that in a few hours it would be common knowledge in every hamlet of the globe whether the men of the *Titanic* went down in stoic, silent heroism or in panic and fear," wrote the *Lewiston Evening Journal.*

"As the story was unfolded later, it was different than had been expected. The one thing which stuck out, unchanged from first wireless dispatches, was that the old law of the sea, 'Women [and children] first,' was lived up to, even though at times it was necessary to invoke the authority of a pistol's muzzle."

At midnight, after the paper had been put together, a group from the *Lewiston Evening Journal* went out for a quick snack at the Owl Cart. There they found a large crowd, and all were talking about *Titanic.* There were expressions of sympathy, but the main focus of the discussion was whether the ship had sunk all the way to the bottom of the ocean.

Things were also in full swing at the *Portland Evening Express.* Friday was Patriot's Day, which usually meant a day off for the staff. "Friday was anything but a holiday to the employees of the

Evening Express. . . . Instead of a holiday, it became a day of record-breaking activity in the [newspaper] office."

The editors made every arrangement to cover the story as thoroughly as possible. At 11:30 a.m. on Friday, they put out an extra twenty-two-page edition that contained approximately thirty columns of news regarding the wreck. "And such news! The news at first hand! The news the people had waited for since Monday morning."

Eva Shorey, a staff writer for the Portland paper, had been sent to New York earlier in the week, the paper having obtained permission for her to be among the first to interview the survivors of the *Titanic* as they disembarked from the *Carpathia.* The management thought it best to send a woman to cover a story that involved a boat loaded mostly with women survivors.

"We think Miss Shorey's story speaks for itself in this connection," said the *Portland Evening Express.*

V

GROWN MEN WEPT ALOUD
—Eva Shorey, reporter,
Portland Evening Express

On Wednesday, April 10, *Titanic* had left Southampton, England, among cheers and well wishes. She was the newest, largest ship in the world, with both the richest and poorest passengers, and everyone in between. She was fresh and new, just like the springtime weather that graced the launching. Passengers on board were going to their homes, both old and new.

The voyage was described as perfect. For Bar Harbor's Madeleine Astor, however, nothing was going right. She was keeping a secret from the public—a public that was being quite hostile to her. Society would find out soon enough when her five-month pregnancy was noticed. Even if enough time had passed since their wedding day, her pregnancy would only serve to fan the fierce fires of gossip ignited by her marriage to John Jacob Astor.

First Class stewardess Violet Jessop would be one of the first to become aware of the feelings Madeleine was keeping inside when Mrs. Astor boarded *Titanic*. "We felt the thrill that the unknown always gives, when we screened that list and found world-famous names but, as yet to us, merely names. We speculated if their owners would tally with our conception of them," wrote Jessop. "So it was not surprising when John Jacob Astor brought his bride of a year on board, about whom there had been so much publicity. Instead of the radiant woman of my imagination, one who had succeeded in overcoming much opposition and marrying the man she wanted, I saw a quiet, pale, sad-faced, in fact dull young woman arrive listlessly on the arm of her husband, apparently indifferent to everything about her. It struck me for the first time that all the money in the world did not make for inward contentment."

The Astors were the most prominent passengers on *Titanic,* but they were little seen until the end. They focused on small, private gatherings during the voyage, such as holding small teas in their stateroom, where they spent most of their time with Colonel Astor's Airedale terrier, Kitty, who never left the colonel's side.

The Astors had left New York in January for Europe, and accompanying them on part of their trip was Margaret "Unsinkable Molly" Brown. The Astors went to Europe aboard *Olympic,* where their personal friend J. Bruce Ismay was a fellow passenger. It was said that Ismay gave up his suite so that Mrs. Astor might be more comfortable. Aboard *Titanic,* Astor would ask Captain Smith and Ismay how the ship was behaving.

They were both from Maine, but their first meeting took place more than five hundred miles away from the Pine Tree State, in the middle of the Atlantic, aboard *Titanic.*

Helen Churchill Candee from York, Maine, and Edward A. Kent, a native of Bangor, met over a copy of *Atlantic Monthly.* Kent had devised this ploy ahead of time, sending a stack of magazines by way of a steward to this woman whom he had not yet met, but knew about through mutual friends.

"Beg pardon," said Kent with a bow as he found Mrs. Candee with his magazines in the First Class lounge, "but I have the April

Atlantic. Is that sufficient introduction, considering Jimmy told me to look you up? My name is Kent."

The two spoke briefly of their mutual friend, of guardian angels, and riddles. He offered his services as an escort, and then bowed himself away.

Kent and Candee had more than Maine in common. Both were successful professionals in their fifties, and unattached. Kent was a never-married bachelor, and Mrs. Candee was divorced.

Born in New York City, Helen Churchill Candee was an author, educated in private schools in New Haven and Norwalk, Connecticut. Although she was a resident of York, as her parents had been, she was truly a world traveler. She was divorced from Edward Willis Candee, who died a few years before the *Titanic* voyage, thus allowing Mrs. Candee to identify herself as a widow. She wrote *An Oklahoma Romance,* and in her 1906 book, *Decorating Styles and Periods,* she used a photograph of a Jacobean chair taken in York in 1902. *The Tapestry Book* was published the year *Titanic* sank, in 1912.

Though Candee was on the largest and most glamorous ship in the world, it was not her love of travel that had put her there. Instead, she was traveling home to be with her son, Harold, who, adventurous like his mother, had been injured in one of the country's first airplane accidents.

Kent's profession was architecture. He was a native son of Bangor, born there in 1854, the son of Henry M. and Harriet Farnham Kent. His family roots ran deep in the state. His mother was born in Winthrop and taught Sunday school at the Unitarian Church in Bangor. His parents ran a popular Bangor retail store, and were described as people of character. Kent had one brother and two sisters, and was active in the Universalist Unitarian Church.

Kent studied architecture at Yale before continuing his studies in Paris for three years. Upon returning to the United States, he first opened an office in Chicago before settling in Buffalo to pursue his profession, at which he excelled. An architect of distinction, Kent designed what were then some of Buffalo's largest buildings, including his father's department store, the Toronto Board of Trade building, the Jewish synagogue, and many residences. His brother William designed the Pearl Building at the corner of Bangor's State and Harlow streets, in 1910.

In 1912 Edward Kent traveled to Europe during the winter, as was his custom. This trip would be different, however. When he returned home after this voyage, he would be retiring. He purposely delayed his return so that he could be on the maiden voyage of *Titanic*.

During the crossing on the *Titanic*, Kent was Candee's first acquaintance, but not the last. Soon Candee and Kent would be at the heart of a small group that spent a great deal of time together, including a historian their age, Colonel Archibald Grace, from the family that gives the New York mayor's mansion its name. Then came Englishman Hugh Woolner, a few years younger than the group, along with James Clinch Smith and Mauritz Björnström-Stefansson.

When she was alone, Mrs. Candee enjoyed time on the deck, where stewards waited on her. "I always take two chairs, one for myself, the other for [friends who call], or for self-protection," wrote Candee in a story describing the voyage. She would not be alone on deck very often, however, for after Mrs. Candee got settled each day, the newly formed group of friends would soon assemble, one by one, using her extra deck chair, the footrest— whatever it took to get close to the attractive widow.

One morning she left her cabin early, planning to explore the ship on her own. She was impressed by the ship's personality, her spirit. Candee called *Titanic* "a monarch of the seas," whose indifference to mankind was significant in its utter self-absorption. "It was only at the bow that I could appreciate her pride in her size. How grand she was, how sophisticated," Candee wrote. "I was sure she liked her name. It suited her. *Titanic,* the biggest ship afloat."

Candee's time with Kent left her intrigued by what she called his look of nostalgic subtle weariness. "Which kind of man was he, the humorous one or the sad?" she asked herself. "Was it apathy, or discontent that made him so unlike the others?"

Their conversations could veer from frivolous to serious in an instant. He talked of the serious business of crossing the Atlantic on a steamer—too serious a business for the frivolity of dressing for dinner, he felt, which is why he did not follow the custom.

On deck, Candee would sometimes see Captain Edward J. Smith and the head of the White Star Line, J. Bruce Ismay, at the railing of the ship, congratulating each other on the speed of the new ship. "Kent would say they should not look so happy on a voyage across the North Atlantic," Candee said.

The same James Clinch Smith of Candee and Kent's social group was also acquainted with the Spedden family, fellow passengers on board the doomed ship. The Speddens, independently wealthy, spent their summers at Grindstone Neck, Winter Harbor, Maine. Frederic was a banker, and his wife, Margaretta Corning Stone, known as "Daisy," dabbled in photography and kept a diary of her daily doings. They lived at the Tuxedo Club in New York, spent their winters abroad, and their summers at the Bonsall Taylor cottage at Winter Harbor. Spedden owned and sailed the *Water Witch,* one of Mount Desert Island's original knockabouts. Their only son, Douglas, seven years old at the time of the voyage, had a nurse named Margaret Burns. He called her "Muddy Boons," as he could not pronounce her name. They were also accompanied by Helen Wilson, the family maid.

Like many children, little Douglas had a favorite toy, a stuffed bear named Polar. Polar was not just any toy; he was a small white polar bear made by the famous Steiff Company of Germany, bought for Douglas at FAO Schwarz in New York City.

Douglas took Polar along on his world travels, keeping him close at hand whether playing inside or out. He built furniture for Polar, who also had his own wardrobe. One time at Winter Harbor Douglas accidentally left Polar on the beach, only to rescue the bear from being swept out to sea at the last minute. On an island near Portugal, Polar stayed with a measles-covered Douglas in quarantine. In the winter, Douglas would push Polar around in a sled. At Christmas, Polar would be served his own holiday turkey dinner, at a table "Master" had built for him.

The winter of 1912 would find the Speddens in Algiers, in Northern Africa. They celebrated George Washington's birthday with a red-white-and-blue-themed tea party. From Algiers they went to France for a month, where Douglas saw his first airplane. Douglas hated to leave France, but was excited to be sailing aboard the magnificent new ship. *Titanic*'s doctor for the First Class passengers, who knew the Speddens from the Adriatic, kissed Douglas on their arrival and said, "I see you still have Polar with you, little man."

Douglas had a good time on the ship. The Verandah Café was the unofficial children's playroom during the day, where Douglas would play with other children. He would send Polar sailing down the banister of the grand staircase. He spent his days on the upper deck, where an iconic photograph would be taken of a carefree Douglas playing with a top, watched by his loving parents. It was an idyllic time for young Douglas.

Sunday, April 14, 1912, the date *Titanic* would hit the iceberg, was a typical day for Mrs. Candee, Mr. Kent, and their group. They all met on deck, where Kent slipped into Candee's extra chair with a gentle yet sure intention. This day was colder than the others, and soon the six retreated from the cold into the First Class lounge, where Kent made a point of sitting beside Candee on a sofa.

Though the group was carefree and gay, Mrs. Candee often had to rein in her worry over her son, Harold, to whose sickbed she was returning. Mrs. Candee would leave the group for her bridge game, and later again for a nap. The group would come together again, for dinner. This evening was so cold that the group decided to stay inside, heading to the à la carte Ritz Restaurant for drinks after dinner, before turning in. The restaurant stewards specially arranged tables to seat the large party.

By now many tables in the Ritz restaurant were empty, most passengers having returned to their cozy cabins, warmed by electric heaters. One party remained, however. The Widener family had been hosting a dinner for Captain Smith. Their dinner party on the night of the sinking was one event that stood out during the voyage. Hosted by Bar Harbor summer residents George and Eleanor Widener, in honor of Captain Smith, it was the place to be that night. It seemed that anyone on the ship who was anyone was there. Guests included Mr. J. Bruce Ismay, Colonel John Jacob Astor, Mr. Charles Hays, Mr. and Mrs. John Thayer Sr., and Major Archibald Butt.

The Wideners, in their fifties, occupied the cabin suite C80–82. They were accompanied on the voyage by their son, Harry, as well as George's valet, Mr. Edwin Herbert Keeping, and Miss Amalie Henriette Gieger, Mrs. Widener's maid. Widener was one of the leading financiers of the country, his father a well-known tractor magnate. George and his wife Eleanor had been in Europe buying art, while Mrs. Widener also supervised the purchase of a trousseau for her daughter, also named Eleanor, who was about to marry Mount Desert Island summer resident

Fitz Eugene Dixon, their engagement having recently been announced.

On Friday, July 31, 1896, sixteen years before *Titanic* sank, a big, new, black yacht called the *Josephine* had steamed into Bar Harbor at 2:30 p.m. On board were Mr. and Mrs. Widener, along with his parents, Mr. and Mrs. Peter Arrell Brown Widener, and Hannah Josephine Dunton Widener. The elder Mr. Widener, sixty-two years old at the time, was principal owner of the Philadelphia Traction Company and a director of the White Star Line, eventual owners of *Titanic.* Mr. Widener also had interests in street railway systems. Also in the party were George Widener's sister and her husband, as well as George and Eleanor's son, Harry, and George's brother and his wife. They were to stay a week, guests of Bar Harbor summer colonist George J. Gould.

The yacht was named after the elder Mrs. Widener, and had left Philadelphia the week prior for a cruise along the Maine coast, with Bar Harbor as its destination. This would be the family's first visit to the island, and a pleasant week was expected to be spent with the Philadelphia colony, well-represented in the popular Maine summer resort. Many small events had been planned to welcome the Widener family to Bar Harbor.

Shortly after the yacht left Philadelphia, however, Josephine Widener became violently seasick, suffering a great deal on the trip from Newport to Bar Harbor. This was nothing new for Mrs. Widener; she had a heart condition, and had not been well for several months. No trouble was anticipated, however, and the trip continued. The yacht docked in Bar Harbor on Friday, and Dr. J. Madison Taylor was summoned from off the island to treat Mrs. Widener for her stomach trouble.

When Dr. Taylor checked with Mrs. Widener again at 9:30 on Friday night, she told him that she felt greatly relieved. The family retired that night, reassured by the improvement in her condition.

The elder Mr. and Mrs. Widener occupied adjoining berths in a stateroom described as beautiful, fitted especially for Mrs. Widener. Upon awakening at seven a.m. on Saturday morning, Mr. Widener went to check on his wife, only to find her lifeless. Dr. Taylor was again quickly summoned. After an examination, he determined she had been dead for approximately five hours. He pronounced her cause of death to be heart disease.

Bar Harbor's Philadelphia circle was shocked. The island undertaker, Mr. Sherman, prepared her body for transport. The remains were enclosed in a beautiful catafalque, laden with many flowers, tributes from friends. At two p.m. Saturday, the *Josephine,* her flags lowered, her cheery colors hidden, slowly sailed out of the harbor. The ship was described by those who saw her as the picture of sorrow. The *Josephine* went to New York City, where a special train took the body back to Philadelphia.

Also at the Widener dinner on the night of April 14, 1912, were Mr. John Thayer and his wife, Marian Longstreth Morris Thayer. Thayer was second vice president of the Pennsylvania Railroad. Their son Jack, born on Christmas Eve in 1894, did not attend the dinner.

Young Jack Thayer occupied a stateroom adjoining his parents' on C Deck, but, being seventeen years old, he was all over the ship. He spent most of the day of the sinking walking around the decks with his parents, chatting with other promenaders. Years later, Jack recalled a short visit with Ismay, as well as a visit with Thomas Andrews, the ship's designer, and fellow railroad man Charles M. Hays. The railroad group spent a lot of time together on the ship.

The afternoon of Sunday, April 14, was noticeably cold for *Titanic*'s passengers. That day Ismay showed the Thayers a wireless message that contained an ice warning, one of many the ship received that day. The Thayers went to their staterooms at about

6:30 p.m. to dress for the Widener dinner party. Young Thayer dined alone. After dinner, Jack put on his overcoat and strolled around deck. He found it had become even colder, and the boat deck was deserted and lonely. Still, it was beautiful. "It was the kind of a night that made one feel glad to be alive," said Thayer.

Friends of the Thayers were Bar Harbor summer colonists Arthur and Emily Ryerson, who embarked at Cherbourg, France. Arthur Ryerson, sixty-one, was from Philadelphia, as were the Thayers. He was on the voyage with his wife and their teenage children, Emily Borie Ryerson, John Borie Ryerson, and Suzette Parker Ryerson. Daughter Ellen Ryerson was not in the party, but instead was back home. They were accompanied by their maid, Miss Victorine Chaudanson, and their governess, Miss Grace Scott Bowen.

The Ryersons were prominent members of the Mount Desert summer colony. Mr. Arthur Ryerson was one of the oldest members of the Mount Desert Reading Room, known also as the Oasis Club. This was Bar Harbor's first social club, formed in 1874 in a small house on the corner of School and Mount Desert Streets. A crudely made sign that said oasis was posted above the front door. During the Prohibition era, this was a place where summer visitors could get an alcoholic drink. In 1881 the club moved to the shore and became the Mount Desert Reading Room, its chartered mission being to promote the literary and social culture of the area. The building still stands today. When the Bar Harbor Reading Room gave its first dance in 1915, there was an objection to the ladies using the ground floor for their entrance, so a special outside staircase was constructed.

The reason for the Ryersons' voyage was not a happy one. They had been touring Europe in their motorcar when they learned that their son, Arthur Ryerson Jr., had been killed in an automobile accident while a student at Yale. The Ryersons quickly booked passage aboard *Titanic*. Arthur's funeral was to be held as soon as the Ryersons returned to the United States.

Mrs. Ryerson typically avoided the deck during the day, but at dinnertime would walk up and down the promenade with her husband. Mrs. Ryerson had been in her cabin all day Sunday, the day of the collision with the iceberg, when early in the evening, Mrs. Thayer came to her cabin, inviting her for a stroll. Mrs. Ryerson agreed, and this was the first time Mrs. Ryerson had gone up in the daytime. The two friends strolled together, and after the walk, at approximately six p.m., the two sat down by the companionway on A Deck. The sky was pink. Mrs. Ryerson's husband talked to Mr. Thayer separately. When the men's conversation ended, J. Bruce Ismay came along the deck.

Mrs. Ryerson had crossed paths with Ismay several years before, and they had several friends in common. Ismay asked Mrs. Ryerson if she found her staterooms comfortable, and if she had everything she wanted. Ismay had given them an extra stateroom and an extra steward to help accommodate their large party. Afterwards, he produced a telegram from his pocket and handed it to her, saying, "We are among the icebergs."

Mrs. Ryerson saw the word *Deutschland* on the telegram, which was a request for assistance. The *Deutschland* had no power. Ismay said, "We are going to get in [to New York early] and surprise everybody," adding that they did not have sufficient time to delay in order to aid other steamers.

Mrs. Ryerson asked Mr. Ismay if the proximity of the icebergs would cause the *Titanic* to proceed more slowly.

"No, we will go faster," replied Ismay, absentmindedly putting the telegram in his pocket.

Mrs. Ryerson said Ismay talked of lighting more boilers, which Ismay later denied. The conversation was confirmed by fellow passenger Mrs. Mahala D. Douglas of Minnesota.

"I carried on the conversation merely to keep the ball going, [although] the words have faded from my mind. [. . .] [T]he strong impression left on my mind I can remember perfectly, but not the words," Mrs. Ryerson said before a Senate committee investigating the sinking.

After about ten minutes Mr. Ryerson and Mr. Thayer came along, and Ismay moved on. Mrs. Ryerson talked to her husband on the way down the stairs about the fact that they might arrive in New York late Tuesday night.

Not invited to the Widener dinner party, but sitting near them in the à la carte restaurant, was Greenville, Maine, summer sportsman and fisherman, William Thompson Sloper, twenty-eight at the time of *Titanic*'s voyage. He was a member of a prominent family from New Britain, Connecticut, the son of a bank president. He was returning from a three-month European vacation at the time of the voyage.

Sloper had what seemed like an idyllic childhood. His father was successful, and his mother stayed at home to care for him. His mother died when he was twenty-six, in August of 1910, a year and a half before he sailed on *Titanic*. He had a brother, Harold Thompson Sloper, who was married with three daughters, one of whom was named Ella, in honor of Harold and William's mother. In the summer of 1911 William's father announced he was going to remarry. His fiancée, Miss J. Myra Wilcox, was a teacher, and twenty-two years younger than the groom. In 1914 they had a child, Erwin Wilcox Sloper. William also had another brother named Kenneth, from his father's first marriage.

"Father did very successfully the necessary 'bread-winning,' and he always was a kind and considerate husband. Mother attended efficiently to all the domestic details of the home. In my later life, after she died and it was too late for me to do anything about it, I often regretted that my two brothers and I always accepted everything which she did for us without giving her in return hardly any demonstration of our appreciation or affection," said Sloper.

Sloper wrote in a telegraph to his brother: "I am on the maiden voyage of the new SS *Titanic,* arriving in New York Wednesday morning. Beautiful steady ship. Hope you will meet me and look her over." The message was delivered Monday morning.

After sending the message Sunday evening, Sloper returned to the ship's library and sat at a desk to write thank-you letters to London friends with whom he had just visited. As he wrote his first letter, fellow passenger Dorothy Gibson approached him, saying that she, her mother, and a New York gentleman were seated across the room, and hoped he would join them as a fourth for a game of bridge.

Gibson was a popular actress, starring in weekly film serials much like *The Perils of Pauline.* The four played through the evening at a table set up for them by a steward in the middle of the library. At ten p.m., while they played, Captain Smith and Ismay passed their table on their way back from the Wideners' private dinner. In the same party that passed the table were also Major Butt, Colonel Astor, and Charles Hays. Sloper said that the party, contrary to rumor, was perfectly sober.

Kent pointed out Major Archie Butt to Mrs. Candee and the rest of his group, noting that he was an aide to President Taft.

"He always seems to know who people are," thought Candee.

Major Archibald Butt was a personal aide to the president, and had accompanied him on a visit to Maine less than two years earlier. Butt had ingratiated himself with the Maine people during that visit. When Taft and his party had arrived in Eastport, Maine, on Monday, July 18, 1910, Major Butt ensured that the party was efficiently distributed into the proper automobiles. He was praised for his tact and for the easy way he handled the arrangements.

"At times, not only in Eastport, but at the other places visited, it became necessary for him to change the plans of local committeemen, but the way in which he did it caused no bitterness, and made all feel that he was one of the best sort of men they had ever met," said the *Lewiston Evening Journal.*

In Eastport Taft enjoyed a full schedule of events, departing on the morning of Wednesday, July 20, headed to Bar Harbor, arriving at three o'clock. They landed at the slip of the Mount Desert Reading Room, the club which Mr. Ryerson had helped to establish. There, President Taft would receive an official welcome from town selectmen. The group was entertained at the Kebo Valley Golf Club between five and six p.m. on Thursday, July 20. One hundred invitations were sent out for the occasion. From there the presidential party, consisting of six people, including Major Butt, went to the Jordan Pond House for dinner.

A company from Boston had been hired to make Bar Harbor presentable for the presidential party. "The streets are being made ready for the occasion, and when the party arrives one will not be able to recognize the beautiful town," wrote the *Bar Harbor Record.* The Seal Harbor correspondent for the paper also wrote about preparations for the presidential visit. "In all probability he will be driven through the village proper, so it would be advisable for all to have their bunting and Stars and Stripes ready for Thursday evening. . . . Seal Harbor is one of the most patriotic little villages about here, and the President will undoubtedly be given a royal welcome."

Taft stayed on the island for three days, after which he was driven in a special car to Bangor, where he gave an address. From there he would return to Ellsworth to spend the night as a guest of Senator Eugene Hale. Taft also visited Islesboro, Camden, Rockland, and Portland during this trip. "At each of these places

Major Butt was the man who was first met and who finally settled all plans for entertainment." In Portland, Major Butt escorted Mrs. Taft and the other women in the party, whom he took shopping.

"The President's aide was a good-looking military man of about thirty-six years of age. He was of medium height, inclined to be slight, but active and pleasant of speech and manner. All those who met him on his visit to Maine in 1910 became very fond of the man, and their sorrow at the news of his probable sad fate at sea will be that of men and women who have learned of the death of a personal friend," said the *Lewiston Evening Journal*.

The Hays party left Montreal on February 12 and sailed from New York on February 18. They went to England, meeting Thornton and Orian there. While in England, Mr. and Mrs. Hays received word that one of their daughters was having difficulty with her pregnancy. This is what prompted them to book their return passage on *Titanic*. On board the ship, Hays spent time with other First Class passengers who were also in the transportation industry. Ismay said he talked to Hays quite frequently during the voyage.

Colonel Archibald Gracie, a member of Candee and Kent's group, told of a conversation he had with Hays the night the *Titanic* hit the iceberg. "One of the last things Mr. Hays said was this: 'The White Star, Cunard, and the Hamburg-American lines are devoting their attention and ingenuity [to] vying one with the other to attain the supremacy in luxurious ships and in making speed records. The time will soon come when this will be checked by some appalling disaster.' "

As Sunday evening wound down, some guests of the Wideners' dinner party were leaving the à la carte restaurant. Other passengers lay in bed, while still others sought to see the day out in the public areas. None heard, shortly after 11:30 p.m. on Sunday night, the sound of three rapid gongs of a brass bell hanging from the forward crow's nest as they sounded out a warning.

"Iceberg right ahead!" called one of the lookouts.

Responding to orders from the officer on watch, Quartermaster Robert Hichens turned the wheel hard-a-starboard, holding it over as far as it would go. The engines were ordered to be reversed, which they were, but not in time. In the thirty seconds that passed, *Titanic* would only veer 20 degrees to port before the impact with a long-warned-about iceberg occurred. The iceberg, caring not about the prominent passenger list, nor the families left behind, left a trail of small yet effective damage extending three hundred feet along *Titanic*'s hull.

Captain Smith, in his ready room after the Widener party, quickly arrived on the bridge. He ordered the engines to stop, then to go half ahead, but soon thereafter signaled a final stop to the engine room.

Mrs. Astor had not been feeling well on Sunday, and had retired early. Colonel Astor had returned from the Widener dinner party and had also retired by the time the ship hit the iceberg.

Mrs. Astor was awakened by the shock of the collision, which she said was rather slight, and by the feel of the engines stopping. Colonel Astor told her it was nothing, and that the engines would start again soon, which they did, although they quickly stopped again. Astor looked out the window and said there was ice about, and that the air was very cold. He dressed and went to the deck to consult with Captain Smith, who said it was serious.

Meanwhile, Mrs. Astor called her maid and put on a light dress, planning to follow her husband. Before she could leave the cabin, however, he returned. Astor's face was grave, yet he was reassuring. "He was very calm, and so I was not alarmed," recalled Mrs. Astor.

However, two women next to the Astor stateroom said they were awakened by the noise of Mrs. Astor outside of her cabin, who, they said, was in a rather excited state.

Their separate suppers complete, at about eleven p.m., Jack Thayer went below to his stateroom and had a short conversation with his parents. He said good-night to them and went to his room to put on his pajamas, "expecting to have another delightful night's rest like the four preceding." Jack again called "good-night" to his parents in the next room, and opened his port window to get fresh air. The breeze came through like a quietly humming whistle. He felt the steady pulse of the engines and propellers. He wound his watch, noticing that it was 11:45 p.m.

"Mother and I were about to go to bed when we were thrown headlong to the floor of our stateroom. Before we knew what had happened, terrible screams seemed to come from every direction."

When Mrs. Widener left the dinner party she had cohosted, Mrs. Candee found that she was the lone woman remaining in the à la carte restaurant, which made her self-conscious—a feeling that another round of drinks could not alleviate. When her watch read nearly eleven o'clock, Mrs. Candee said good-night to her own group, including Mr. Kent, and made for her cabin.

Mrs. Candee asked her cabin steward to direct the bath steward to draw a hot bath, which, she felt, would warm her up and put her mind at ease. She dressed in a thick flannel robe over her nightgown and stood in her cabin, awaiting word that the bath was ready. She wondered what was taking the steward so long. Mrs. Candee happened to be holding on to a post in the middle of her cabin when the crash came. It was this post that allowed her to keep her balance as *Titanic* made its rendezvous with the iceberg.

Mrs. Hays and her daughter Orian Davidson were in their cabins when the crash came. Their husbands were up on deck, engaged in conversation with other passengers. After feeling the shock, Mr. Hays and Thornton Davidson went to see the ice, accompanied by Major Peuchen, a well-known Canadian military officer. They immediately saw that the ship was listing to starboard, which impressed upon them the seriousness of the situation.

Frederic and Daisy Spedden were in their cabin when they were awakened by a sudden jolt and a grinding noise. They felt the engine stop.

Muddy Boons quickly dragged Douglas from his warm bunk, saying that they were taking a trip to see the stars. Daisy and Frederic collected a few toiletry articles and jewelry in a shopping bag, locking their trunk from whence the items came. Frederic took charge of the keys. The Spedden party was prepared when the passengers were ordered to put on their life jackets, and they quickly headed up to the deck with extra blankets. Muddy grabbed Polar from the belongings holder on the wall beside Douglas's bunk before fleeing the room.

Mrs. Ryerson was awake at the time of the collision. Unlike her husband, who was sleeping soundly, she was unable to sleep because of the cold. She heard the engines stop but felt no collision. She rang the steward, asking him what was the matter.

"There is talk of an iceberg, ma'am, and they have stopped, not to run into it," he said.

She asked the steward to keep her informed if there were any orders given. Because of the cold, she put on a warm wrapper and looked out the large cabin window that she had on B Deck. It was midnight. She was greeted by shining stars, a calm sea, and no noise. After about ten minutes she went out to the corridor and saw people hurrying about.

At 11:30 p.m., ten minutes before the ship hit the iceberg, the library steward had asked the Sloper party to finish their bridge game so he could extinguish the lights and retire. It was then the party noticed they were the last ones left in the room. They counted their scores and left at 11:40 p.m.

At the top of the stairs, Miss Gibson said she would like to take a quick walk around the promenade deck before going to bed. Sloper suggested they go to their rooms and don warmer clothing, planning to meet back at that location once they were ready. Sloper hastily went down a flight of stairs to his room, where he put on a hat and overcoat. He returned, and while waiting for Gibson, he looked at a map of the Atlantic Ocean that hung in the companionway.

"Suddenly the ship gave a lurch and seemed to keel over slightly to the left," Sloper later recalled.

Henry Sleeper Harper, forty-eight, owned Turtle Island in Frenchman Bay, off Mount Desert Island. He was a grandson of John Wesley Harper, one of the founders of the Harper publishing business. He and his wife, Mrs. Myra Haxtun Harper, forty-nine, occupied cabin D-60. With the Harper party was Mr. Hammad Hassab, twenty-seven, of Cairo, Egypt, who had been Harper's guide on his European winter vacation.

Harper had stayed in his stateroom during the voyage due to a case of tonsillitis. At the time of the crash he was awakened by a grinding noise that seemed to come from below the deck. Although he had been in a shipwreck previously, he thought they had simply run over a fishing shack. He sat up, looked out the window, and saw an iceberg only a few feet away, moving away at high speed and crumbling as it went. He knew what this meant.

"Get dressed quickly," he told his wife. "We must get up on deck."

Still weak from his illness, he dressed slowly. Mrs. Harper dressed more quickly and went for the ship's doctor, hoping he would convince her husband to stay in the cabin. According to Harper, the doctor told him to undress and go back to bed.

"Damn it, man, this ship has hit an iceberg," Harper said to Dr. O'Loughlin. "How can you say there's nothing serious?"

The doctor asked Harper to stay put while he investigated.

A few minutes later Dr. O'Loughlin returned.

"They tell me the trunks are floating around in the hold," said the doctor. "You may as well go on deck."

VI

Within fifteen minutes a ship's officer had made a tour of the ship. Flooding was discovered in the forward boiler room and the Orlop deck, near the mailroom in the bowels of the ship, where postal clerks were already busy hoisting heavy bags full of mail to a higher deck. At 12:15 a.m. the position of the ship was quickly calculated, and a distress call was made over and over by the ship's two wireless operators. They flashed MGY, the call letters of the ship, followed by CQ, meaning the message was for all ships, and the letter D, meaning distress. Captain Smith and Thomas Andrews, the ship's designer, went below to see the damage for themselves. Before long Andrews made the deadly assessment: The ship had two hours, at most, to live.

Officers and crew assembled on the ship's bridge, and soon the order went out via word of mouth—there being no public address system or alarm—for all passengers to report to the boat deck with life jackets on. On deck, steam being forced from the now-closed boilers made a deafening sound that pierced the frigidly cold Atlantic night. Outside the First Class lounge on A Deck, the ship's orchestra played popular music.

Second Officer Charles Lightoller was preparing the lifeboats to be launched. Realizing there was not enough room in the lifeboats for everybody—not even enough room for half the people aboard—Captain Smith gave the fateful order: "Women and children first."

Colonel Astor took his young pregnant bride to the boat deck. They found everything extremely quiet. They walked around, and soon people began pouring up on deck. The excitement was growing, but the ship seemed all right. The order was then given to get on the lifeboats, but no one wanted to do so.

When Hays, Davidson, and Major Arthur Peuchen went forward along the ship after the crash, they were confronted with the sight of ice on the forward well deck. The ice crunched under the feet of those who were walking on it.

Mrs. Hays and Mrs. Davidson were told there was no danger, and were directed up on deck as a precaution. Mr. Hays and Mr. Davidson returned to their cabins to get their wives warmer coats.

Between the time of the impact and the party's wait to board a lifeboat, Hays talked to another passenger, who said the ship had plenty of time left. "This boat is good for eight hours," Hays told his wife. "I have just been getting this from one of the best old seamen, Mr. Crossly [Crosby]."

Mrs. Candee let go of the post in her cabin after the shock had subsided. She was sure the ship had run over some subsided mountain. In fact, she fully expected to see the mountaintop when she opened the cabin door to see what was going on outside.

Instead she found silence, and loneliness. The lights in the hallway burned an unimaginable light she had not seen before. There was not a human being in sight. The strange light, and the sense of loneliness, were at the heart of this moment for Mrs. Candee.

She called for the steward, but there was no answer. Finally he came to her aid from the deck below. She asked what had happened; why had the engines stopped?

He replied that there was nothing to worry about. He told her that she should go back to her cabin and go to bed—that her presence in the hallway would frighten the other passengers. She replied that she had traveled enough to know something was wrong.

After the steward left, alone in her cabin, she contemplated her next move. The steward's dismissal of her concerns left her weary. She had seen the anxiety on his face, and wondered what he had seen below. She knew she could not sleep, so she dressed herself for a walk on deck. She went down the passageway, noting the strong illumination, the absence of people and, again, the silence.

One of her group, Hugh Woolner, soon arrived, and arm in arm, they made their way up to the topmost deck, the boat deck. She was amazed by the beauty of the natural scene: the sky full of stars lighting the glassy surface of the ocean, a complete scene with no skyline to break the unity.

"It was like the inside of a globe," she thought at the time.

Mr. Harper put on his overcoat, Mrs. Harper her fur coat, and they, along with Hassab and their Pomeranian dog, headed for the deck. The Harpers would go up one flight, stop and rest for a few minutes, because of Mr. Harper's weakened condition, and then go up another flight of stairs. By the time they got to the gymnasium on the top deck, they saw men and women standing about in groups, talking. Mr. Harper noticed no excitement; everyone just seemed curious. "Everybody seemed confident that the ship was all right," said Harper. "She certainly *seemed* all right."

A steward came along and said the ship would be delayed for about two hours, and that the passengers should return to their quarters.

"They dropped away a few at a time—casually drifted off," said Harper.

Still, there were a few dozen people left near Harper. Word was passed around that the passengers should put on their life belts. Then came a long wait. Harper was surprised that no officer was around to give them any further information, or to tell them what to do next.

"We were left to ourselves," said Harper. "I was pretty sore by that time, and I think anyone would [have been] who knows anything about seafaring."

Eventually a steward came around, calling for women to go to the lower deck. Some went on their own; some were escorted by their husbands. Mr. and Mrs. Harper simply looked at each other and continued to sit and wait. Soon stewards and other men of the ship's company began fumbling with the tackle of the lifeboats near the Harpers. "They seemed quite unused to handling boat gear," said Harper.

As the ship crashed into the iceberg, Dorothy Gibson came running up the stairs to reunite with William Sloper, and the two of them went out to the promenade deck on the starboard side.

"Peering off into the starlit darkness, we could both of us see something white looming up out of the water, rapidly disappearing off the stern," said Sloper.

Because of the coldness in the air, they determined that they must have struck a glancing blow with an iceberg. Sloper suggested that Gibson tell her mother what had happened, and then they could have their walk.

At about 12:15 a.m., the bridge party of four was assembled on A Deck and heading toward the stern. They rounded the corner by the smoking room and started back toward the head of the ship. At about the middle of the ship Sloper asked the other three if it also felt to them like they were walking downhill. "When they agreed that we were, I think we all realized, without saying anything, that the bow of the ship must be settling in the water quite fast, because it had been less than half an hour since the ship struck the iceberg," Sloper recalled.

They went back inside the foyer outside the smoking room and found thirty or forty other passengers, most of them dressed in nightclothes and dressing gowns. Thomas Andrews, the ship's designer, came running up the steps three at a time. Miss Gibson approached him, put her hands on his arm, and demanded to know what happened. "Without answering and with a worried look on his face, he brushed Dorothy aside and continued on up the next flight of stairs to the top deck, presumably on his way to the captain's bridge."

A moment or two later one of the bedroom stewards came by, following Andrews. With a raised voice, the steward called out, "The captain says that all passengers will dress themselves warmly, bring their life preservers with them, and go out onto the top deck." The foursome headed for their staterooms to get their life preservers, promising to meet again in the same spot before fulfilling the captain's orders.

"Returning for the second time to my warm, brightly lighted cabin, where my room steward before dinner had laid out on the other bed my dinner suit and dress shirt, I got my life preserver down out of the overhead rack, still not believing that I wouldn't soon return to the room to go to bed," said Sloper.

"Put on your life belts and come up on the boat deck," a passenger said to Mrs. Ryerson.

"Where did you get those orders?" she asked.

"From the captain," the passenger replied.

Mrs. Ryerson told Miss Bowen and her daughter, who were in the next room, to dress immediately. She then woke her husband and her two younger children in a room on the other side of hers. She then remembered her maid, who had a nearby room. The maid's room was locked, and Mrs. Ryerson had a hard time waking her. When Mrs. Ryerson returned to her own room, her husband was fully dressed. They could hear the noise of feet tramping on the deck above them.

Mrs. Ryerson found her husband to be quite calm and cheerful. He helped his wife put life jackets on the children and the maid. Because of the large number in their party—seven—Mrs. Ryerson was quite afraid of not getting on deck together, and in time. In order to speed up the process of family readiness, Mrs. Ryerson simply put a fur coat on her younger daughter. With calls from Mr. Ryerson to stick together, the Ryerson party went to A Deck, finding a large group of people they knew already there, including the Astors, Thayers, and Wideners.

"Everyone had on a life belt, and they all were very quiet and self-possessed," said Mrs. Ryerson.

Young Jack Thayer quickly put his overcoat back on, along with his slippers. He called to his parents that he was going back on deck "to see the fun." His father said he would dress and soon join him.

On deck, it was bitterly cold. Thayer walked around, looking over the side of the ship. He saw nothing except for ice scattered on the forward well deck. There were only two or three people on deck when he arrived, but soon many more had gathered, including his father. They finally found a crew member, who told them the ship had hit an iceberg. The ship started listing to starboard. After about fifteen minutes, the ship began listing to port, and was noticeably down by the head.

"No one yet thought of any serious trouble," said young Thayer. "The ship was unsinkable."

The Thayer men went below to find Mrs. Thayer and her maid fully dressed. Jack Thayer quickly dressed, putting on a warm greenish tweed suit and vest, with another vest, mohair, underneath his coat. He tied on his life preserver, over which he wore his overcoat.

The Thayer party then headed to the lounge on A Deck, which they found crowded with people, some of whom were standing still, some hurrying, and some pushing their way onto the deck. It was noisy. The band was playing lively music, which the worried passengers did not seem to notice.

Jack Thayer said his mother was unnerved by the accident. Deckhands shouted that there was no danger, which calmed many. "Men and women were running in all directions, and everyone was excited. Women fainted," said Jack Thayer.

Knowing that the order had been given for women and children to be first to board the lifeboats, the Thayer men left Mrs. Thayer and her maid with the group that included the Astors, the Ryersons, and the Wideners. Now just past midnight, the two Thayer men went inside the ship. People stood around, dazed, questioning each other about what had happened. No one seemed to know what to do. They saw Ismay, Andrews, and some of the ship's officers walk by. It was then that Andrews told the Thayers he did not give the ship much more than an hour to live.

"We could hardly believe it, and yet if he said so, it must be true. No one was better qualified to know," said Jack Thayer.

"Each face reflected the sign he had seen, the sign of coming death," said Mrs. Candee. "Each one knew what the passengers did not know."

On the boat deck, Candee and Woolner idly discussed the stars, the surrounding chatter calming her nerves. Candee watched as the captain ordered the lifeboats to be lowered to A Deck, one deck below, for loading. She listened to the sound of wood on wood as the boats were released from their chocks, and the sound of creaking pulleys as they used the ropes to do the job.

Candee and Woolner made their way down to A Deck, where it was discovered that the unbreakable safety glass in the large square windows was preventing passengers from getting to the lifeboats, hanging just out of reach. The captain ordered the boats back up to the boat deck. The group of Bar Harbor millionaires—the Astors, Thayers, Ryersons, and Wideners—followed, by way of a crew-only set of stairs, up and down between the boat deck and A Deck, chasing the elusive Lifeboat 4, which, had it not been for the glass, would have been one of the first to be launched from the sinking ship.

Knowing that the lifeboats would soon be lowered, Candee and Woolner made their way back down belowdecks so she could dress in warmer clothes. As they moved down the stairs, people started moving to the upper decks, glancing at Candee quickly, as if she were moving the wrong way. Back downstairs, the passageways were no longer empty. People milled about in their nightclothes, slowly, with curiosity. One man gave a piece of ice to Mrs. Candee, who accepted it hesitantly.

Kent stood at the bottom of the stairs, maintaining a brave face but somehow still signaling dire meaning with his sensitive features. "How like the gentle Kent not to burden anyone with his feelings," thought Candee.

Passengers now had on their life vests, which Candee and Kent found out was per the captain's orders. Björnström-Stefansson joined the group as they made their way to Candee's cabin. The steward was already there, waiting for her.

As the steward laced her boots, Candee picked up a small toiletry case. Kent, who was now looking in her cabin door, reacted with horror, telling her she could not take any baggage with her. Candee had not thought of the small case as baggage.

Inside the case was a small miniature of Candee's mother; the rest of her jewelry was already carefully stored throughout her inner clothing. She held her beloved cameo out to Kent, asking him to take it, feeling it would be safer with him. She reasoned that being a man, he would have a better chance at survival. She was hurt when he refused to take it. She also offered him a silver pint flask. Finally, he silently took the items, but his reaction made her wonder about the future of the ship and her passengers.

She shook the steward's hand as she left. Kent silently slipped away from the group as Woolner and Björnström-Stefansson escorted Candee to the upper decks.

William Sloper and the other three members of his party met again in the same spot on the starboard side, headed to the topmost boat deck. It was lit up by floodlights that Sloper said had been erected during the voyage for celebrating *Titanic*'s New York arrival. The sound of steam escaping from the funnels was deafening. The group was unable to hear their own voices as they helped to tighten each other's life belts.

They watched as the first officer and some sailors lowered some of the lifeboats to deck level. By now fifty or sixty passengers were assembled on deck, and the first officer, holding a megaphone to his mouth, announced, "Any passengers who would like to do so may get into this lifeboat. There will be no difficulty launching it, as the sea is perfectly calm. Later, after we have had a chance to find out how much damage has been done to the ship, we will pick you up again."

Some passengers got into Lifeboat 7, while some stepped aside, all done calmly. "Every passenger seemed to have taken a firm grip on his nerves," said Sloper—all except for Miss Gibson, who had become quite hysterical, and kept repeating loudly, "I'll never ride in my little gray car again."

Sloper, with the help of the first officer, helped Dorothy down into the bow of the lifeboat, while Mr. Seward and a junior officer helped Dorothy's mother in. Dorothy would not let go of Sloper's hand. "We won't go unless you do," said Gibson. "What do you say?"

According to Sloper, the officers then helped Sloper and Seward into the boat. They sat for about ten minutes, looking at the faces of passengers on deck who were trying to make up their minds whether to also get in. Nineteen more people embarked.

"Are there any more who would like to get into this boat before we lower it away?" asked First Officer William Murdoch through the megaphone. When no one else came forward, the officer gave the signal to lower.

"Then began the jerky descent to the surface of the ocean, about sixty feet below," said Sloper. The trip was uneventful. Theirs, Lifeboat 7, was the first launched, at 12:45 a.m., an hour after *Titanic* had struck the iceberg—an hour and twenty minutes before *Titanic* would sink.

Mrs. Candee and her group—minus Kent, who had left to seek provisions for the lifeboats—returned to the boat deck. She could see the scene was now changing from what it had been just moments before. People were pouring onto the top deck. At some point armed guards blocked the entrance to the deck. The captain ordered Woolner and Björnström-Stefansson to accompany Mrs. Candee to Lifeboat 6. As they escorted her over to the boat, the confused-acting captain shouted at them again.

"Hey, you two—come away from that boat! No men are allowed near the lifeboats."

The two men dropped Candee as if she were a leper. Candee entered the boat herself, quickly lost her footing after stepping on the oars, and fell into the boat, injuring her ankle.

The lifeboat filled slowly. Mrs. Candee watched as several married couples came up to the lifeboat, only for the women to decide against getting in, not wanting to leave their husbands. At the time, Mrs. Candee thought that staying aboard the ship might be the safer option.

"The *Titanic* was the entire world," she said, recalling her thoughts at the time. "A place of serenity." But, she realized, she had been ordered into this lifeboat by the captain, and in the boat she would stay.

At 12:55 a.m., ten minutes after Sloper's boat had left the *Titanic,* the crew on deck started lowering Mrs. Candee's lifeboat. Mrs. Candee called it a casual affair until, during the lowering, in the loud din, one seaman held his side steady while another lowered his, leaving the fragile craft dangling from one end. The passengers slid down, precariously close to spilling into the Atlantic's freezing water seventy feet below.

"Hold up forward," Candee shouted up to the deck.

Once the lifeboat hit the water, she discovered there was only one man in it: Quartermaster Hichens, who had been at *Titanic*'s wheel at the time of the collision. "We've only one man in this boat," she hollered up to Second Officer Lightoller. "Only one man."

A yachtsman volunteered to lower himself down the ropes to assist. The captain also threw in a boy, who was disabled in the fall. As the lifeboat neared the water, Mrs. Candee saw rows of lit portholes underwater. It was then that she realized the ship was sinking.

"All boats row away from the ship," shouted Captain Smith repeatedly to Candee's lifeboat. "All boats keep together."

Due to the lack of men, the women had to help handle the oars. Soon the freezing weather had an effect on the lifeboat's passengers. Mrs. Candee shared her extra furs, but found she could not help many of them. They mostly went to a beautiful young woman clad only in a silk opera wrap with just a nightgown underneath. "I felt like scolding her," said Candee. "There had been plenty of time to dress fully and in street clothing."

In this lifeboat were two key witnesses to the disaster: Hichens, who had been at the wheel at the time of the crash, and Frederick Fleet, one of the lookouts, who had been in the crow's nest. There seemed to be a lack of official leadership in the lifeboat. Hichens, who took command of the lifeboat, took a steamer blanket from one of the women. He spoke dire words to his charges, reminding them that they were 1,200 miles from land, with no food or water. He added that they did not even know in which direction they were headed.

"We are going straight north," Mrs. Candee called to him in anger.

"How do you know?" he taunted.

"There is the North Star directly above our bow," she replied, which shut him up.

The passengers on the boat deck gathered and watched the ship's crew at work. Mr. Harper looked over the lifeboats and chose Lifeboat 3 on the starboard side. He handed his wife down, and she comfortably seated herself. Others got in, including his dragoman, who had accompanied them so that he could "see the country all the crazy Americans came from," along with their dog.

Five stokers suddenly jumped in the forward part of the boat.

"Huh!" exclaimed the seaman in charge of the boat. "I suppose I ought to go and get my gun and stop this."

"Everybody seemed to take what was happening as a matter of course, and there wasn't a word of comment," said Harper.

Frederic Spedden went up to the boat deck, saw lifeboats being lowered, and came back down for his party. They stood at the foot of the stairs. The Speddens saw no widespread panic, but one hysterical woman was quickly taken away. They waited for orders while a steward gave a few last-minute adjustments to the party's life belts and ordered that the blankets be left behind, saying they would just be in the way.

They found that Lifeboat 3, Harper's lifeboat, was clear of the deck. Daisy Spedden said that short-legged people had to practically be thrown in because of the distance of the boat from the ship.

Charles Hays and his son-in-law Thornton Davidson also put their wives into Lifeboat 3.

"We were told there was no danger, and that the boat at the worst would float for days, and that other ships were rushing to our rescue," said Mrs. Hays. "The women were told to get into lifeboats and that the men would be safe. There was no panic or confusion. The sea was as calm as a millpond, and the sky was clear."

A Grand Trunk Railway official later recounted more of Mrs. Hays's story for the press: "The men wrapped the ladies in their warm fur coats, and with Mrs. Hays's maid helped them into the boats. The last that the wife and daughter of Mr. Hays saw of him, he and Mr. Davidson . . . were standing on the deck, waving to the ladies in the boat."

The women were convinced that the men had no idea the ship would sink because they were so confident in her. Still, Mr. Hays told his wife and daughter he thought they should enter a lifeboat, saying that he and Davidson would stay aboard the ship until help came in the morning. Mr. Hays called out to his wife,

"The *Titanic* is good for ten hours, and by that time help will surely have arrived."

"We did not think of even kissing them a good-bye," said Orian Davidson.

Mr. Harper got in and sat with the stokers. No one was left on deck. He had on his arm his little brown Pekingese spaniel named Sun Yat-sen that the Harpers had picked up in Paris, named after the Republic of China's first president. The dog kept very quiet. The seaman in charge ordered the boat to be lowered. The groups of men at each end of the boat handling the falls let out some line, and the boat was lowered clumsily, first going down by the head, then the stern, as had happened in Mrs. Candee's boat five minutes earlier. The boat held no food, water, or lantern. Two men lost oars over the side.

"It was all done by hand, and very clumsily done," said Harper.

A passenger from Second Class climbed down the ropes and joined the group in the boat. When they reached the water, the boat crew did not know how to release the ropes. While they worked with the ropes, the lifeboat grated against the side of *Titanic.* After a while they were released, and the crew began rowing.

"And such rowing!" said Harper. "You've seen the young man who hires a boat on Central Park Lake on Sunday and tries to show off. Well, about like that, skying the oar on every maneuver, burying the blade on the pull or missing it altogether."

At Lifeboat 8, on the port side, stood Dr. Alice Leader, a middle-aged widow from Lewiston. She had been traveling with a party of four, and was about to retire on Sunday night when she heard the crash and felt a pronounced jarring of the ship, which was over in moments. With other passengers she made her way to the deck to see what was the matter.

Dr. Leader, forty-nine, was born in New York and was a physician in Lewiston, Maine, for seven years, building up a large practice with her husband, Dr. John Leader, also a physician. The *Lewiston Evening Journal* credited her womanly sympathy and kindness as a reason for her success as a physician: "She was always responsive to the needs of the poorer class of people with whom she was thrown in contact, both professionally and otherwise, and among these people in Lewiston she was always much beloved. . . . She is a woman of scholarly attainments, of broad interests, and of great ability in her profession."

Dr. Leader's husband died in October 1900, and after a few months she decided to relocate to New York City, where she took a job at the Roosevelt Hospital and became a member of that city's board of health. She also started her own private practice there.

Miss Nellie Leader of Lewiston, Alice's sister-in-law, had received a letter from the widowed physician telling of her plan to return home on *Titanic* after a three-month trip to Europe.

Dr. Leader later recalled the moments after impact with the iceberg: "The deck was covered with ice, but it did not occur to me that there was the slightest danger." A gentleman standing nearby was "apparently divining our thoughts," and said to her, "There is danger; the other end, the baggage rooms, are flooded."

"We all knew that we were in danger, but believed the *Titanic* unsinkable," said Leader.

The ship gradually settled in the water and listed to port. Dr. Leader went up to the boat deck, where she saw the crew launching lifeboats. "Get into the boat," said her friends, and she did. She was wearing warm clothes, but could see others in the boat were not. "Some of the ladies were only in their nightdresses and slippers," said Dr. Leader.

The group made up of the Astors, Thayers, Wideners, and Ryersons, among other passengers, were denied a quick escape from the sinking ship because of the locked A Deck windows that Mrs. Candee and her companion had pointed out to Captain Smith. Lifeboat 4 would have been one of the first launched were it not for those locked windows. Because of this blocked access, the group of Bar Harbor millionaires was one of the last to leave.

With the safety glass preventing their entrance into the already-lowered lifeboat, the group was ordered back up to the boat deck, where crew members would raise Lifeboat 4 back into position for loading. This had yet to happen, so the group was waiting there.

Colonel Astor sat on an exercise horse in the gymnasium on the boat deck next to his wife and her maid, Rosalie. With a pocketknife, he cut into a life belt to prove how sturdy it was, and held out the pieces in his hands. Madeleine helped him tie on his life belt. She said he was cool and collected, and his only thought was her comfort.

Mrs. Ryerson's maid ran back to the cabin to get more clothes, and soon returned. Mrs. Ryerson's primary thought was not to make a fuss—to do as they were told. Mr. Ryerson joked with some of the women he knew. The ship's crew fired rockets while the group was on the boat deck. It was after one a.m.

"They wouldn't send those rockets unless it was the last," Mrs. Ryerson said to her husband. She begged him to stay with them, but he replied, "You must obey orders. When they say 'Women and children to the boats,' you must go when your turn comes. I'll stay with John Thayer. We will be all right."

Mr. Thayer and his son had said good-bye to Mrs. Thayer on A Deck, leaving her with the group, thinking she would be put off the sinking ship in the lifeboat. Young Thayer and his father walked around for a while, then decided to check to make sure Mrs. Thayer had made it off safely. They met a steward in the main dining room who told them she was not off yet. The steward took them to her.

Reunited, the Thayers waited briefly on the boat deck before the group was ordered back down to A Deck, where the elusive Lifeboat 4 still awaited them. By now the device to open the window had been found. The group headed down a set of crew-only stairs, but a crowd of people got between young Thayer and his parents. Once Jack Thayer could get through the crowd, he looked for his parents, but they were gone.

The ship by now was only twenty minutes away from sinking, and the scene on *Titanic*'s sloping decks was growing chaotic. The Bar Harbor group waited their turn as they watched other passengers getting into boats. The sense of desperation was growing. The ship's crew used a cable to pull Lifeboat 4 closer to the ship, which was at a distance because of the dying ship's distinct list to port. Mrs. Ryerson was confronted with a crude set of steps, made up of a deck chair, to get from the window to the boat, hanging a few perilous feet away from the side of the ship.

Mrs. Ryerson had her son, Jack, with her. Second Officer Lightoller said, "That boy can't go." Mr. Ryerson stepped forward. "Of course that boy goes with his mother; he is only thirteen." Lightoller let him on, at the same time giving the order, "No more boys." Mrs. Ryerson turned, kissed her husband, and left him with Mr. Thayer and Mr. Widener as she boarded the boat. The trio of men stood together very quietly.

Stepping through the window, or having been flung by a ship's officer, Mrs. Ryerson went from the lit deck to darkness, falling onto the women already in the boat. She scrambled to the bow with her eldest daughter, while Miss Bowen and her son were placed in the stern, her second daughter in the middle with her maid. People piled into the boat quickly, some thrown in.

At this point, the *Titanic* had only minutes left to live.

VII

An officer took Mrs. Astor by the arm and made her get into a boat, although she did not want to leave without her husband. The colonel told her he would join her, as there were several empty seats. Astor handed his wife into a boat tenderly and then asked permission to accompany her due to her delicate condition.

"No, sir, not a man shall go on a boat until the women are all off," First Officer Lightoller said to Astor.

One survivor, Nicola Yarred, an immigrant, said Astor loaded in his wife, then looked back to the deck and saw others wanting to get aboard. He picked up the first person he saw—Nicola herself—and placed her into the lifeboat.

Miss Margaret Hays said the colonel was in the boat and a woman came running down the deck. Astor raised his hand to stop the boat's lowering. Mrs. Astor cried out to be let out of the boat with him, and he spoke to her privately.

"The ladies will have to go first," Miss Hays heard him tell his bride.

Mrs. Astor would later deny the rumor that Colonel Astor had tried to enter the boat. Colonel Gracie said Astor had held his wife's arm as Lightoller lifted her into the boat. He confirmed that Astor had asked permission to enter the boat because she was in a delicate condition, a request which Lightoller denied. Gracie did not believe Astor ever tried to enter the boat. Gracie said that all of Astor's energy was spent in rescuing his wife.

"The conduct of Colonel John Jacob Astor was deserving of the highest praise," said Gracie.

According to George A. Harder of Brooklyn, Mrs. Astor was tearful. Astor tried to put a young boy in the boat but was refused, the officer saying "Women only." Astor picked up a discarded woman's hat from the deck and placed it on the boy's head and brought him back to the boat. "Here, little girl, climb in," Astor said to the child, and the officer let him in.

Just before the lifeboat was launched, a man fought his way through the throng of people on deck and jumped into the boat. Other passengers also started jumping in as the men were trying to lower the boat. Lacking enough seamen to handle the boat, one of the officers sent another seaman down the ropes.

Mr. Ryerson and George Widener were standing behind the rail of the *Titanic,* both waving their arms, throwing kisses and calling farewell to their wives and children. Astor calmly stepped back and lit a cigarette. He called to his wife to ask if she was comfortable.

"Good-bye, dearie—I'll join you later," said Astor. "The sea is calm and everything will be all right. You are in good hands, and I will meet you in the morning."

Mrs. Ryerson said she saw two lines of portholes, then just one, as the ship sank further into the freezing water. She saw water washing in the portholes, over the gold furniture and decorations. "I could see all the portholes open and water washing in, and the decks still lighted," said Mrs. Ryerson.

It was 1:55 a.m. when the millionaires' boat was launched the twenty feet that now stood between the water and A Deck. Ten minutes later, the stern lifted noticeably from the water, the ship's forecastle almost completely underwater. The band began to play "Nearer, My God, to Thee." The bow went under, the stern rose, and the smokestacks started to come loose, falling among the people in the water. The lights suddenly went out. As the ship started its trip to the ocean floor, the sound of everything falling and boilers exploding filled the air, and then everything was suddenly silent.

Mrs. Candee's attention was called back to the sinking ship. One by one, the rows of lights went under. One woman in her lifeboat went mad with grief for her son.

In Candee's boat, Hichens chose to lash their lifeboat with others, but the disturbance of the water from *Titanic*'s sinking made the water turbulent. As they fiddled to separate the boats, the *Titanic* sank.

"No one spoke. Speech was insufficient for such a catastrophe," said Mrs. Candee. "Then did hope drop from me. The whole world was gone. The beautiful effulgence was gone with the ship, and I was alone in the dark."

As the ship started to go under, Hichens ordered the passengers to row as hard as possible.

"Hurry," Hichens ordered. "Otherwise we won't make it. She's so large that when she sinks, she'll pull everything down for miles around," he growled.

The male passengers of William Sloper's lifeboat were ordered to get out the oars that were stowed along the sides, and row. Sloper said that he sat beside a sailor in the bow of the boat and helped him to maneuver the small boat away from the sinking ship. He said the three sailors in the boat were concerned about getting away quickly lest they get caught in the suction of the ship if it started to go down fast.

"So for the next half-hour the three sailors, with some help from passengers, clumsily maneuvered the lifeboat for a quarter-mile away from the ship . . . for the next hour and a half we just sat there and drifted farther and farther away." By the time the ship sank, Sloper said the sailors estimated the boat had drifted two miles away.

While they waited for salvation, the boat took ten people from an overcrowded lifeboat that had been launched later than theirs. They distributed a bundle of rugs thrown into the boat by an officer just before it launched. Miss Gibson, dressed in a summer evening dress with only a sweater and polo coat, was feeling the cold. Sloper lent her his heavy woolen winter coat, recently completed by a London tailor. He still had on a heavy Shetland wool V-neck sweater.

Sloper said *Titanic* stayed lit until almost the end.

"Then suddenly, like the house lights in a brilliantly lighted theater just before the curtain goes up, all the lights on the ship dipped simultaneously to just a pale glow. A moment or two later everyone watching in the lifeboats saw silhouetted against the starlit sky the stern of the ship rise perpendicularly into the air from about midship. Then with a prolonged rush and roar, like the sound of ten thousand tons of coal sliding down a metal chute several hundred feet long, the great ship went down out of sight and disappeared beneath the surface of the ocean. Then a great cry arose on the air from the surface of the calm sea where the ship had been: a cry from the throats of 1,600 people who had been thrown into the water from the decks of the ship as she went down," said Sloper.

Sloper said some of the screams came from what he thought were frightened people afloat on hastily inflated pneumatic life rafts: "[T]heir massed voices would rise and fall in a tremendous wailing crescendo which reverberated off into the starlit darkness of the silent night."

Henry Harper estimated that there were about forty people in his lifeboat. There was only a little bit of moon in the sky. From the deck of the ship he heard several bursts of cheering, which he figured was the sound of people hearing the news that rescue ships were on the way. The boat's crew rowed in circles, heading the boat into the side of the ship. Harper barked at them.

After about an hour the lights on the ship went out suddenly. Harper knew her end was near. He heard a roar and hissing coming from the ship. "No one in our boat said a word, but I feel sure the seriousness of the situation began to depress everybody," said Harper.

Slowly the giant black hull began to diminish against the sky-line.

"It was a frightful thing to feel that the ship was going, faster and faster, and that we could do nothing for the people on her," said Harper.

Harper said not a sound came from the ship until the very last, when a sort of wild maniacal chorus, mingling cries and yells, arose from the ship. The crew began to row as hard as they could away from the sinking ship. There was no talking on the boat, just the sound of the oars in the oarlocks.

"These were the most awful moments in the whole experience," said Harper. "Bravery was shown by the people in every phase of the emergency, but flesh and blood could not withstand that gasping cry of horror as the sea rose to them."

Dr. Leader's lifeboat was lowered without mishap. It was 12:30 a.m. when her boat got into the water. By now the lower decks were flooding. There were twenty women in her boat and only two men. The women joined in with the rowing, escaping the stricken liner. She said she saw the iceberg that had struck the ship visible in the starlight.

"It stood high out of [the] water and was a terrible spectacle," said Dr. Leader.

For the next hour and a half, Dr. Leader and the others in the boat watched the lit ship and heard music from the orchestra. The music eventually faded away and the lights disappeared.

They were a mile away when the ship went beneath the waves for the final time. They watched the rockets go up. Dr. Leader described how the ship sank more and more, until she broke in two, the rear half landing back in the water. Dr. Leader recalled that for a few minutes, "[although] it seemed to be an eternity," loud cries filled the air. They would go silent, and then they heard only the splash of the waves against the side of their small boat.

"No one can realize the agony of those minutes when the screams and cries for succor from those who had been swept from the decks into the sea were borne to our ears by the ice-cold breeze of the night," said Dr. Leader. "Never, so long as the good God permits me to live, will I ever forget those cries!"

Soon the cries were silent.

"As the prayers and screams for help ceased, we all knew what it meant," said Dr. Leader. "Death had relieved them of [their] agony and suffering."

Everyone in her boat said a prayer for those who had gone down with the ship.

During the lowering of Mrs. Astor's lifeboat, the ropes stuck and the boat tipped. With the *Titanic* nearly sunk, the trip to the water for the lifeboat was short—only twenty feet, compared to seventy feet for the other lifeboats. It was then Mrs. Ryerson realized how far the ship, now just minutes from going under completely, had already sunk.

The boat pulled away and almost immediately gained water, until it was up to their knees. Mrs. Astor bailed water. They picked up six men, two of whom died immediately after being pulled aboard.

Mrs. Ryerson said there was confusion in the orders, and for that reason they did not make much progress in getting away from the ship. Someone ordered something about a gangway, and the boat started pulling for the ever-rising stern of the ship. "No one seemed to know what to do," said Mrs. Ryerson. She could see her younger daughter, along with Mrs. Thayer and Mrs. Astor, rowing. She said they all did this clumsily, except for Mrs. Astor.

The lifeboat was caught in a whirlpool. Still near the ship, Mrs. Ryerson realized it was now sinking rapidly. Barrels and chairs were being thrown overboard, threatening the safety of their small craft. "I was in the bow of the boat with my daughter and turned to see the great ship take a plunge toward the bow; the two forward funnels seemed to lean, and then she seemed to break in half as if cut with a knife."

The lights on the great ship went out, and the stern stood up for several minutes, "black against the stars," and then plunged down. "[A]nd then began the cries for help of people drowning all around us, which seemed to go on forever. Someone called out, 'Pull for your lives, or you'll be sucked under,' and everyone that could rowed like mad."

The *Titanic* was pitch-black. After the ship sank, Madeleine Astor thought she heard her husband calling for her. She stood up in the boat and cried that they were coming, but the others in the boat made her stop.

Jack Thayer watched as the last two starboard forward lifeboats were loaded. A large crowd of men was pressing to enter them. He saw Ismay push his way into one of them. Men jumped from a higher deck into the boats, and officers shot at them with revolvers.

"It was really every man for himself," said Thayer.

The lifeboats were all gone, including the four collapsibles stored on top of the officers' quarters on the topmost boat deck. Passengers from Second and Third Class now clogged the decks, along with the remaining First Class passengers. Crewmen stood and waited for orders. One man emerged on deck with a full bottle of Gordon's gin, which he put to his mouth and practically drained. This was one of the first men Thayer would see on the *Carpathia*.

People seemed to be standing as far away from the rails as possible, which were exposed to the sea after the lowering of the lifeboats. Young Thayer would later learn that his father was among a group of men standing near the second funnel, which is close to where he now stood.

At 2:15 a.m., he could see the water coming up the deck, the ship sinking rapidly now. He thought of the times he would never spend with his parents again, or his sisters and brother. "I sincerely pitied myself," Thayer recalled.

As the water came up the deck, the crowd pushed to get higher, at the end of the ship. "We were a mass of hopeless, dazed humanity, attempting, as the Almighty and Nature made us, to keep our final breath until the last possible moment," said Thayer.

He stood by the railing just aft of the captain's bridge. He made up his mind three times to jump but could not do it, afraid of being stunned when he hit the water. The ship started to move forward, moving into the water at an angle of about 15 degrees. Thayer threw off his overcoat and climbed over the rail, sliding down, facing the ship. Thinking his parents must have gotten off safely, Thayer made a jump for it right before the ship sank. Thayer plunged down into the water, spinning in all directions.

Underwater, Thayer was pushed to the surface by a strange force, believed to be an exploding boiler. Facing the ship, he saw one of the four giant funnels fall into the water, landing about fifteen yards away from him, a mass of sparks and steam coming out of it. He floated among the wreckage until he was almost frozen to death before catching hold of a big stick of wood.

Thayer continued to think of his father, and those thoughts numbed his physical pain.

Thayer would later reach out and feel the cork of an upturned lifeboat, one of the two of twenty that had not been properly launched. The men on top of the flat-bottomed craft helped the young man on. He sat on his haunches, facing the *Titanic.* He saw the black mass of people still on board, continuing to the stern. Her forward motion had stopped, and now she was pivoting at a point near the middle of the ship. Her stern gradually rose in the air, slowly, deliberately.

"She then seemed to rise in the air and stopped at an angle of about 60 degrees," Thayer recalled. "It seemed to hold there for a time, and then, with a hissing sound, it shot right out of sight, with people jumping from the stern."

The mighty *Titanic* having sunk, those in the lifeboats turned to the fight for life.

After the ship sank, Candee knew the time had come to take action. The sounds of more than 1,500 people screaming for help filled her ears.

"We must go back," she cried out.

"No," replied Hichens. "It is our lives now, not theirs. We would go to our own deaths."

In the boat, there was the sound of quiet sobbing and the heavy rhythm of the oars. Mrs. Candee sank into a heavy, almost unconscious dumbness. "If I sit here for one more minute, I'll utterly freeze to death!" cried Candee.

They quickly found they were surrounded by ice.

The heartbreaking silence when the more than 1,500 voices went silent, along with the feeling of utter loneliness, cast a deep gloom over Lifeboat 3.

In the lifeboat, Mrs. Hays and her daughter would call out, "Charles Hays, are you there?" There would be no answer. Despite their grief, Mrs. Hays and her daughter asked one woman to sit closer to them to keep her warm. Another passenger in the lifeboat called the two women brave, saying they never lost their courage all night.

According to Mrs. Spedden, the lifeboat made for the lights of a ship in the distance, thought to be the *Californian*. They were unsuccessful in that endeavor. Douglas opened his eyes about three a.m. and said he felt seasick. "[L]ook at the beautiful North Pole, and no Santa Claus," Douglas said as he woke up to the scene.

Muddy Boons told him the story of Cinderella and quieted him back down.

As dawn broke, the occupants of Lifeboat 3 spotted the lights of the *Carpathia* and made for it. The horizon was pink, and the morning glow on the icebergs that filled the scene was beautiful.

Mrs. Davidson offered her straw hat to burn to signal the rescue ship.

Mr. Harper's group sat closely for warmth. When the *Carpathia* arrived, Harper thought how tiny she looked compared to *Titanic*. Still, "I never saw a finer sight than that ship, which had raced through fifty miles of field ice and bergs to come to our rescue." He noted that the icebergs he saw after the sun rose looked as big as the pyramids he had just toured.

Dr. Leader told her story to F. L. Dingley of the *Lewiston Evening Journal* at her home on 118th Street in New York the day she returned.

Dr. Leader described the work of getting their lifeboat to the *Carpathia* as long and hard. They spent the night chasing phantom ships and icebergs that looked like sailing ships. In addition, the seamen in her lifeboat could not row skillfully, and several women—including fellow passenger, the Countess of Rothes—rowed in turn. Most of the women were unfamiliar with the skill of rowing, or had only rowed light crafts before.

"Not one grumbled. It was life they were fighting for. They did their best. Hands were blistered, yet the women rowed in stoic silence, with grim determination, toward that point from which the relief ship was expected to come," said Dr. Leader. "It seemed like dawn would never come. Only those who have been cast upon the great wide expanse of ocean at midnight in a small boat can understand the feelings which held us."

When they saw *Carpathia* at dawn, a glad shout was let out by the occupants of Dr. Leader's boat. They gave a prayer of thanks.

Some of those in Lifeboat 4 proposed to return to the sinking ship and fill the lifeboat, which could have easily held fifteen more people, but some of the women grew hysterical at the idea. They even went so far as to interfere with the rowers. Mrs. Astor insisted that the boat return, but as they approached, the *Titanic* sank. Still, they rowed about and picked up eight men, two of whom died in the stern of the lifeboat, and one of whom lost his mind. The women of the boat did their best to help them, taking off their furs to provide warmth.

"Some of the women protested, but others persisted, and we dragged in six or seven men," said Mrs. Ryerson.

Ernest Person recalled that Mrs. Astor pleaded he be taken into the lifeboat on which she was a passenger. His wife and daughter perished in the sinking. He also lost his sister and niece by a swell during the sinking, which also carried him off the boat. He was holding on to a plank in the water. "Please let them get in. They have as much right to live as we," Mrs. Astor reportedly said to the crew, regarding Person and others who were clinging to an overturned lifeboat.

A twelve-year-old boy reported that he was pulled from the water by the Astor lifeboat, and that Mrs. Astor saved him by warming him under her clothing because he was wet and freezing. She also prevented the crew from throwing him overboard after he was pulled in from the water.

A member of the ship's crew, fireman James Crimmins, said he was half-naked when they pulled him from the water. Mrs. Astor ripped her big fur muff down the middle to wrap him in it, which he said saved his life.

On board the bottom of the upturned lifeboat, Jack Thayer and the rest of the thirty men had to get out of the wreckage and away from the swimmers. They were reduced to beating men with boards to keep them from swamping the fragile craft.

On the bottom of the boat, they all grasped at the half-inch overlaps of the boards to keep from sliding into the icy water. As morning grew near, the air escaped more and more from under the boat, bringing them closer and closer to the freezing Atlantic.

The men clung together. They said the Lord's Prayer, sang hymns, and waited for dawn. Because a radioman was on board, they knew that the *Carpathia* should be arriving around 3:30 a.m. As the rescue ship hove into sight, Second Officer Lightoller blew his whistle as the rest of the lifeboats rowed farther and farther from them to safety. The men were eventually unloaded into an under-filled lifeboat.

The seemingly endless ordeal of the sinking had only lasted for about two hours and forty minutes, yet this relatively brief interval had changed the survivors' lives forever.

VIII

Eleanor Danforth of Gardiner, Maine, and her aunt, Eleanor Stevens of Randolph, had a ringside seat to the rescue of *Titanic's* survivors.

On board *Carpathia,* in the wee hours of the morning on Monday, the stewards were mustered and told a wireless had just come in that the *Titanic* had hit an iceberg and probably would need help. They got coffee ready, laid out blankets, and made sandwiches. The captain turned off the hot-water supply to divert steam to the engines.

An English doctor was sent to the First Class dining room, an Italian doctor to the Second Class dining room, and a Hungarian doctor to Third Class. Rope ladders and chairs attached to ropes were made ready. Canvas ash-bags tied to ropes were made ready for hauling up children.

Icebergs were everywhere—twenty-five of them, by most counts, ranging in height from five feet to two hundred feet. Because of them, *Carpathia* could not maneuver to each lifeboat, but instead had to sit and wait for the boats to be rowed to the rescue ship.

Eleanor Danforth, twenty-two at the time of the sinking, was the daughter of Frederick Danforth and Caroline A. Stevens, the youngest of their four children. Her grandfather was Judge Charles Danforth, one of the first board members of the Merchants National Bank of Gardiner. Her father was a civil engineer, and had served as mayor of Gardiner at the turn of the twentieth century.

Miss Danforth got up early on Monday morning, as was her custom, and went on deck, as usual. "We are going to the help of the *Titanic*," she was informed by a steward. At the time it was still dark, but as the day dawned, Miss Danforth could see the gleam of the icebergs that surrounded the ship, and found the scene magnificent but terrifying. *Carpathia*'s sailors were on the lookout for *Titanic*, which was thought to be still afloat at the time. Around four a.m. the first lifeboat was spotted.

"There was no sign of any steamer, and not a vestige of any wreck except the lifeboats when we arrived on the scene," said Miss Danforth. "It hardly seemed possible that such a giant craft could have completely disappeared."

They came upon the first lifeboat quickly. Miss Danforth noted that it was half full of passengers, some in nightclothes. One man wore a dress suit. Some women were bareheaded, some in their evening clothes. "The people in the lifeboat were calm, but their faces were drawn, and all were shivering with the cold," she observed. More lifeboats started reaching *Carpathia* then, in rapid succession, some with women at the oars. Miss Danforth watched as the rescue ship's sailors plucked the dazed survivors one by one out of the lifeboats with a series of ropes.

Early in the morning, a shout came from another lifeboat that had spotted *Carpathia*. A slight breeze had begun to stir, and the water started growing rough.

It took Lifeboat 7—William Sloper's boat—about an hour to row to *Carpathia*. They were the second or third boat to come alongside her. Sloper and his fellow passengers quickly made their way up a stairway which had been lowered down the side of the rescue ship. They spent the next hour or two watching the other lifeboats make their way to *Carpathia* and up the same stairway.

In the predawn darkness the *Carpathia* hove into view. At first Mrs. Candee did not realize the rescue ship was real. "Minds long bruised with strain and anguish do not rise instantly into complete joy," she wrote. "The difference was there; I received the fact with unnatural calm."

Hichens, in charge of Candee's lifeboat, twisted an oar suddenly, sending the lifeboat directly toward the hull, and a high wave sent them into the side of the ship. The crew of the *Carpathia* in charge of the bosun's chair cursed.

Lifeboat 3 came alongside *Carpathia,* and a chair rigged to a whip was let down to unload the passengers. According to Mr. Harper, the third woman to leave, a woman of substantial size, was stepping forward to take her place when, to the amazement of all in the boat, another woman, clad only in a nightgown and kimono, sprang from nowhere and sat up on the floor of the lifeboat.

"Look at that horrible woman!" the other woman cried, pointing to the large woman in the chair, who looked astonished. "Horrible! She stepped on my stomach. Horrible creature!"

The woman in the kimono was the next woman to be hoisted to safety.

When it was Harper's turn to go, he got in the chair and found himself hoisted aloft quickly. A pair of hands kept him from bumping his head against the ship as he made his ascent. When he arrived on deck, one man seized ahold of Harper, another wrapped a warmed blanket around him, and a third assisted him into a room, where he was served a cup of hot coffee and a big drink of brandy. The process took no more than half a minute.

The Speddens were taken up in the chair, young Douglas, in one of the ash-bags used to transport the children. Daisy Spedden found the reception that awaited the passengers overwhelming in its warmth. Coffee, sandwiches, and whiskey were served in the dining saloon, and blankets were distributed for those suffering from exposure.

"From that moment we went on picking them up, and as the rescued came aboard, their thankfulness for safety was always mingled with the sense of their loss and the chattering cold that possessed them," said *Carpathia*'s master, Captain Arthur Rostron.

Carpathia passenger Eleanor Danforth said that some of the women were in a state of collapse when they finally realized they had reached safety. She said some had to be carried into the dining room, and a few became hysterical. Only about five women had to be taken to the ship's hospital.

After the last lifeboat was hauled aboard, the ship circled the site of the sinking, which held no bodies. The sea was nearly empty, with just a bit of wreckage, a few deck chairs, a few life belts, a lot of cork—"no more flotsam than one can often find washed onto a seashore by the tide," said Rostron. He saw only one body.

The women were calm while *Carpathia* looked for further survivors, but at the point the last had been found and no more were alive, "then bedlam came." According to one of *Carpathia*'s stewards, nothing could be done to comfort the women until they had "cried themselves out."

"Many of the women had been hours in those open boats, shielded from the almost arctic cold only by a coat hastily thrown over nightclothes, telling of the urgency with which they had left the ship, suggesting to the imagination awful long-drawn-out anxiety before the slips were loosed and the boat was on the water and away," said Rostron.

Those aboard *Carpathia* held a service in the First Class dining room for those who were lost, and giving thanks for those who were saved.

By eight a.m., after all of the survivors had been recovered, Rostron asked the newly arrived *Californian* to look for further survivors just to be safe, while he made his way back to New York.

Male passengers and officers gave up their cabins. Many ladies doubled up in their accommodations.

It took four hours and fifty-six miles for *Carpathia* to get out of the pack ice.

The *Olympic* wanted to take the survivors on board, but Ismay ordered *Titanic*'s identical sister ship to stay out of sight.

On board *Carpathia,* Mrs. Astor was escorted to the infirmary by the ship's senior hospital attendant. She was given the captain's private stateroom, to share with Mrs. Thayer and Mrs. Cummings, another First Class passenger. Back home, news went about that she was deathly ill. Mrs. Astor did not emerge from her room on *Carpathia* for the entire return voyage.

Vincent Astor sent a cable to his father, originally thought to be aboard *Carpathia:* "Shall be in Halifax with private car Wednesday morning at 8:55. Anxiously await word from you. With love, Vincent."

On April 18, Madeleine sent a cable from *Carpathia* to her mother in New York, stating simply, "Mrs. Astor safe."

Polar, seven-year-old Douglas Spedden's favorite stuffed animal, was left behind in the lifeboat, which was stowed on the bow of the ship along with others. A sailor noticed the toy and took it to a warming table in the kitchen. Douglas soon spotted him, and the two were reunited. By this time Daisy had gotten Douglas a substitute bear from the ship's barbershop, but the replacement bear was soon forgotten.

Almost immediately on board *Carpathia,* the Speddens began to help their fellow survivors. One of those they helped was Colonel Gracie, Candee and Kent's friend, who sat naked, wrapped in blankets on a sofa. The Speddens and Muddy Boons gave him hot cordials and hot coffee, which soon warmed him up and dispersed the cold.

"The scenes in that room were simply heartrending," Daisy said.

To distract Douglas, they sat him in a corner with a plate of sandwiches. One woman who had lost her husband and two children filled the room with dreadful screams. Young Douglas gave his only handkerchief to a weeping woman from steerage.

One man gave up his room for the Spedden family. Daisy found the small quarters quite comfortable, although Douglas said he had preferred their quarters on *Titanic.* Douglas wondered why they had had to go to the lifeboats to see the stars when they could have seen them perfectly from *Titanic.* His parents explained that *Titanic* had gotten a "little wet," and they could not return to her.

The Speddens worked hard that first day looking after their special charges, which included a few steerage passengers. The women of the Spedden party cut up blankets to make clothes for the children of the Third Class survivors. "The scenes down there, and the expression of hopelessness and despair on some of the faces, were heartbreaking to see," said Daisy. Frederic and Daisy went to bed that first night worn out, both mentally and physically.

The next few days of the voyage home were foggy and dismal.

For Mr. Spedden, much of his time aboard *Carpathia* revolved around his duties with the newly formed committee of *Titanic* survivors. This committee drafted resolutions of gratitude to God,

Captain Rostron, and the officers of the *Carpathia.* A collection was organized for the poor aboard who had lost everything. An amount of ten to fifteen thousand dollars was raised on the voyage home.

On April 18 the Speddens sent a telegram to family members in Connecticut: "All safe on *Carpathia.* Notify family and friends. Spedden."

On April 17 a telegram was sent to *Carpathia* for Mr. Hays's son-in-law, Thornton Davidson: "Hearty congratulations! I bet you are a chronic bull on Marconi stock henceforth. Please rush tele-graph [of] your experience."

Like all the others, Mrs. Candee was offered assistance by a crowd of nurses and stewards of Carpathia. "I was actually safe at last," she recalled.

Her ankle pained her and she longed to lie down, but she did not know where to go on the ship. She did not understand the magnitude of the disaster, or that it was such big news back home. She worried that there was a small chance her daughter, Edith, might hear about it, so she arranged for a wire to be sent home. The message was never delivered.

Candee limped into the ship's dining room for roll call. Soon Woolner and Björnström-Stefansson arrived in the room, arm in arm. While Candee's companion Edward Kent had died trying to get food to the lifeboats, Woolner and Björnström-Stefansson confessed that they had jumped into one of the lifeboats while it was being lowered.

One of *Carpathia*'s passengers gave up their room, in which the injured Candee occupied the lower berth. Here she spent her return voyage to New York. The ship's barber donated a tooth-brush, which Woolner brought to her. That was all she saw of him. She shared the cabin with a large female survivor, who wore her dead husband's pajamas. This woman cried all night for a lost string of pearls.

William Sloper would spend the voyage on *Carpathia* writing his own eyewitness account of the tragedy. He said he felt lucky to have taken part in the historic tragedy and to have survived so that he could tell the story. Sloper knew that John A. Gleason, city editor of the *New Britain Herald,* would be glad to have his personal account. When not writing his story, Sloper spent much of his time on deck with Miss Gibson, her mother, and Mr. Seward.

Dr. Leader was very well-traveled, and had been to Cuba, Jamaica, Panama, Trinidad, Barbados, Cherbourg, Paris, and London. She suffered no ill effects from her *Titanic* adventure, but was thoroughly exhausted.

When she had left New York on her trip, she had brought along several large trunks. Arriving home after the sinking, she carried only a small tin ginger box containing a pack of cards and a photograph of the *Carpathia.*

As the sun rose on the morning of April 15, Jack Thayer, perched precariously atop the ever-sinking overturned lifeboat, had seen *Carpathia* as she hove into view. It was then that Thayer knew he would live. He, along with the others on the upturned lifeboat, would be taken into another lifeboat and brought to the rescue ship.

On board *Carpathia,* he awoke to his mother leaning over him, crying. He later recalled what happened next:

"Where is Father?" I asked, but she did not reply.
"I remained until the last, Mother, and tried to be a man. I wanted to stay with him until the end, but could not."
She was overjoyed to see me, but it was a terrible shock to hear that I had not seen Father since he had said good-bye to her.

As Thayer and his mother talked, someone gave him a coffee cup full of brandy. It was the first alcoholic drink he had ever had. "It warmed me as though I had put hot coals in my stomach, and did more too," said Thayer, who slept until noon.

During the voyage home, *Carpathia*'s doctor asked if Thayer might pay Ismay a visit, seeing as his family knew the White Star director so well.

Thayer found Ismay in a terribly nervous condition when he entered the room, the older man not even registering Thayer's presence. The ship's doctor came in and asked if he could get them anything. Thayer replied that he would like some bacon and eggs, which were brought to him.

Thayer told Ismay he had every right to take the last boat, but Ismay continued to stare ahead, without speaking. His hair, which had been black on *Titanic*, had turned virtually snow-white.

"I have never seen a man so completely wrecked. Nothing I could do or say brought any response," said Thayer.

On April 18 a wireless message was received in Philadelphia, signed by Mrs. Thayer. It read: "Jack, Margaret, and I safe. No news of Mr. Thayer." At the time Mr. Thayer's name was still on the list of survivors.

"The trip back to New York was one big heartache and misery," said Jack.

On board the *Carpathia,* Mrs. Hays and her daughter Orian were offered every consideration, and made as comfortable as possible. In vain they sought their men.

Eleanor Danforth was one of many *Carpathia* passengers who sacrificed their staterooms for the *Titanic* survivors. Many hours were spent sewing and planning for the survivors. Men rolled themselves in blankets and slept under saloon tables in the dining room. Others slept on the tables themselves. Chairs were at a premium.

"But no one complained, whatever his lot," said Miss Danforth.

On Wednesday, April 17, *Carpathia* encountered fog, causing the whistle to blow every half-minute, jangling the already-frayed nerves of *Titanic*'s survivors.

When the ship finally headed into port in New York, they were surrounded by news boats. Before they could dock, the weather turned dramatic. The wind blew hard, it rained, and then there was thunder and lightning.

IX

The narratives gathered piecemeal from the liner's 705 survivors pay a tribute without precedent to the bravery of the men and women of these modern days—bravery of impulse, unstudied, unassuming, and instinctive alike in steerage passengers, stoker, and millionaire.

—*Aroostook Times*

Preparations had been completed for *Carpathia*'s arrival. Customs regulations were suspended. Only the relatives of survivors with proper credentials obtained from the White Star Line office would be admitted to the pier. More than a thousand passes were expected to be issued.

Two hundred and fifty policemen gathered early at the Cunard Line piers at West 14th Street and North River in a drizzling rain, among ropes dotted with green lights, stretched for seventy-five yards in front of the piers to hold back onlookers. As early as 8:00 p.m., automobiles containing veiled women and silent men started to arrive, and by 8:30 a crowd had started to gather on the pier.

Everyone talked in whispers, many holding out hope that their loved ones, although not on the official survivor list, might have lived. Across the way a small hotel had been converted into headquarters for the press, and also provided rooms for those who were bereaved, or who had relatives on board *Carpathia.*

Taxicabs had been requested, and hotel accommodations had been made for First and Second Class passengers not able to proceed immediately to their homes. Steerage passengers would be cared for by the immigration department at Ellis Island, or by the Municipal Lodging House, which had been placed at their disposal.

At eight o'clock word had spread that *Carpathia* was passing the Statue of Liberty. By around 8:30 p.m., five hundred friends and relatives had assembled in the pier sheds under alphabetical letters correlating with the last names of the passengers they were looking for. Several Red Cross nurses and twelve physicians awaited the ship's arrival. The Pennsylvania Railroad had a special train waiting for those who wanted to go to Philadelphia.

There were thousands of people in the sheds by 8:45 p.m., many weeping. Automobiles kept piling up. At five minutes to nine the *Carpathia* was there and ready to dock. However, she could not do so until the *Titanic*'s lifeboats had been removed.

A crowd now estimated to be ten thousand strong took up vantage points along the waterfront to see *Carpathia*'s arrival. Silence fell over the crowd as the ship, lit by the photographers' flashbulbs at different intervals, approached the dock. The ship was described by eyewitnesses as looking like a "funeral boat." The ship was warped into its slip among newspaper boats and the flashes of photographers' cameras, which felt "like a series of bombs."

Every ship in the harbor blew its whistle in tribute as *Carpathia* came to dock.

"Her decks were black with passengers, but there was a notable absence of the usual hilarity and excitement usually attendant upon an ocean liner's arrival," said the *Portland Evening Express.* White-clad hospital attendants with stretchers and "invalid chairs" mingled with officials from the coroner's office as the ship docked.

"Lights of the *Carpathia* are now visible from the Battery," was the news item that sent the staff of the *Lewiston Evening Journal* into action, "for what was to be one of the most exciting nights in the newspaper history of the world."

J. P. Morgan was at the pier awaiting *Carpathia.*

The women's relief committee, of which Morgan's daughter Anne was a member, met the rescue ship, sorted clothes, prepared to pass out hot coffee and sandwiches, comforted the stricken women and the frightened babies, and saw them off in buses arranged by Mrs. William K. Vanderbilt.

A hush fell over the crowd and the flash of cameras ceased at the moment the first survivor disembarked *Carpathia,* at 9:35 p.m.

Eva Shorey of the *Portland Evening Express* was also waiting at the pier. Her story would appear in the newspaper's special edition:

STRONG MEN WEEP ALOUD

Agonizing Scenes at the Pier as Titanic's *Survivors Leave* Carpathia

EXPRESS-ADVERTISER REPORTER LEARNS HARROWING DETAILS

Dramatic in the extreme was the arrival of the Cunard liner so eagerly awaited by the whole world. Like a funeral ship of state, the *Carpathia,* with her awful story of the shipwrecked *Titanic,* and bearing the pitiful remnant of the passengers and crew, crept out of the fog and silently came to her dock in New York tonight. A pall of rain added to the gloom. A sob went up all over the city where excitement in all quarters has been at fever pitch and the nervous tension at the breaking point.

Thousands of men, women, and children choked the streets for blocks. Police regulations were unusually strict, and the line of motors and carriages was kept in place, as well as the throngs of surging humanity.

When the survivors began to appear, strong men wept aloud, the hysterical cry of women was heard, and agonized faces looked in vain for the sight of loved ones they would not give up as lost. The reunions were tragic in the extreme, and all in the vast crowd were in one of those emotional stages rarely witnessed. High and low, woman of fashion and the immigrant met on a common ground. Joy and sorrow, happiness and agony and the sympathetic sob over, everywhere apparent.

The scene on the pier was one of wild chaos and emotion. The thunderstorm and resulting downpour only added to the intensity of the experience. The faces of those waiting on the pier were wan and haggard. Some held placards aloft bearing their names, while others stood under the alphabetical letters in the pier sheds. "Hysterical shouts, piercing cries of agony, and groans of pain added to the general confusion," wrote Shorey, continuing her account:

The *Titanic* was literally broken in two by the explosion of her boilers. This is the story told by the survivors who arrived in New York tonight. When she crashed at highest speed into an iceberg, which tore a jagged hole on the starboard quarter, the icy water rushed on the boilers. She sank in two hours and thirty-five minutes from the time she was struck Sunday night.

The strains of "Nearer, My God, to Thee" were heard by those in the lifeboats just before the *Titanic* went to her watery grave. Sixteen boats were in the forlorn procession which entered on the terrible hours drifting. Women wept for lost husbands and sons. Sailors sobbed for the ship which had been their pride. Men choked back tears and sought to comfort the widowed. They strove, though none too sure themselves, to convince the women of the certainty that a rescue ship would appear.

Most heartrending scenes occurred on deck when husbands and wives were separated . . . Mrs. John Jacob Astor was forced from her husband by the officers.

The awful suspense is at last ended.

One of the tragic sights was to see the beautiful Mrs. John Jacob Astor, whose marriage a short time ago was so widely discussed. Her first question when she came on the pier was, "Have the others got in yet?" Her sister and Mr. Astor's son, Vincent Astor, led her to the waiting limousine with murmured words of comfort. The courageous acts of her husband as reported in the press must be a solace in her days of anguish.

The awaiting Astor party, including Madeleine's stepson, Vincent, and her sister, Katherine, waited on the dock for *Carpathia,* along with two doctors, a trained nurse, and an ambulance. The papers had stated that she was very ill, and the Astors had had no word from her, all amid rumors of her dying in the disaster.

Vincent had received permission to board *Carpathia,* to aid Mrs. Astor, and it took him several minutes to force his way through the crowd to do so. He eventually found her and escorted her down the gangplank. Mrs. Astor walked unassisted, wearing a white sweater. The party avoided the crush of people by taking a freight elevator down to the street, where their automobiles awaited them.

"They embraced with tears, hurried to a limousine, and drove to the Astor town house," read the story in the *Bangor Daily News,* compiled from New York wires.

There were three automobiles with the Astor party, with Vincent's big limousine at the head of a long line of awaiting automobiles. Vincent cranked the car himself and jumped into the driver's seat.

"How is Mrs. Astor?" he was asked as he attempted to drive off.

"She is well," he replied. "I am delighted to say that she is far better than I expected to find her."

"Are you taking Mrs. Astor home?"

"We are taking her there directly," Vincent replied.

"Have you any other good news to give?"

"No," he said. "I have not yet dared to ask Mrs. Astor any questions."

"No news of Colonel Astor?"

"No," he replied sadly.

Mrs. Astor was said to be in the best condition possible in light of the circumstances, but was in no condition to discuss the details of her ordeal.

On their way home, the Astor party stopped to see Madeleine's father, Mr. William Force, on 37th Street. He was disabled, and thus unable to meet them at the pier. A member of the family said she visited with him for a few moments and then headed to her own home, the Astor mansion on 57th Street.

Mrs. Astor told the family she did not know what had happened to her husband. She remembered that during the confusion, as she was boarding her lifeboat, Colonel Astor had stood by her side. She said the men hadn't seemed anxious to leave the liner, and that everyone appeared to be in a daze. After that, according to Astor trustee A. J. Biddle, she had no recollection of what happened until the boats were clear of the sinking ship. She said there was room for at least fifteen more people in her lifeboat.

Madeleine Astor was overheard making a few remarks to her father, before she left his home to head to the Astor estate. "I hope he is alive somewhere," Mrs. Astor said. "Yes, I cannot think anything else."

Mrs. Astor held up well until she reached her home, where she broke down for a brief time. True to form, however, she rallied quickly.

"I never saw a sadder face or one more beautiful, or anything braver or finer than the wonderful control she had of herself," said W. H. Dobbyn, an Astor Trust official. "You would be terribly sorry for her if you could see her and hear her tell of the awful tragedy."

Mrs. Astor was described as being "utterly exhausted by her experiences." According to trustee A. J. Biddle, Mrs. Astor was in no physical danger whatsoever after her experience. Just as a precaution, however, her physicians had ordered that neither Mrs. Astor nor her maid were to talk about the disaster.

Later, when interviewed by reporters, Madeleine's father Mr. Force made it clear that no one was to apprise Mrs. Astor of the truth about her husband.

Mrs. Hays and her daughter Orian Davidson were shaken when they arrived in New York, although they both appeared to be in good health. The women were first met by Grand Trunk Railway official Howard Kelly. The party quickly boarded a private train provided by the railway and headed for Montreal. Mrs. Hays and daughter were accompanied on the train by Mrs. Hays's father, W. H. Gregg, her granddaughter, Miss Dyer of Jacksonville, Florida, her brother, Norry B. Gregg of St. Louis, and her sister, Mrs. Ludwig Kotenay, also of St. Louis. Mrs. Hays was described as being in perfect health and seemingly good spirits—at least, as good "as could be expected."

In Montreal, the Grand Trunk special car stopped short of the regular station in order to avoid the public. They were met by Davidson's parents and his brother. Cabs awaited the party, who were whisked home.

A correspondent with the *Portland Evening Express* met the special train that carried Mrs. Hays. "Did you know that Mr. Hays was not among the survivors?" the reporter asked Mrs. Hays.

"I knew that he was not on the *Carpathia,* and that the *Titanic* had gone down," she answered.

Mr. Kelly said he had not put many questions to Mrs. Hays. She had told him there was no disturbance, and that the women were placed in lifeboats, and that Hays and Davidson had helped them into theirs. The last she saw of them, they were standing together on deck. She said it was very dark, and the only indication they had that the ship had sunk was the extinguishing of the lights. Mrs. Hays suffered considerable discomfort from the extreme cold, and she did not know any of the others in her lifeboat. On *Carpathia,* they received every consideration and were made as comfortable as possible under the circumstances.

"I do not think it probable that they realized the fact that their husbands were lost until the following day, although I did not question them directly upon this point," said Kelly.

Mr. Gregg, Mrs. Hays's father, was angry. "We ride on these big ocean liners thinking that everything is provided for our safety," he said. "We look about, see the handsome furnishings and equipment, and feel content that our lives are safe. That these are mere tinsel was shown by the loss of the *Titanic* in a calm sea. Had there been more boats, I am sure everyone would have been saved."

Mrs. Thayer and her party, which included a large group of her friends, left for Philadelphia immediately upon arrival in New York, a special train awaiting her. No one was permitted to address her concerning her experiences.

George Widener's only brother, Joseph, went to New York to meet Eleanor on the *Carpathia.* They had given up hope for

George Widener and his son Harry. Peter Arrell Brown Widener, co-owner of *Titanic,* and father and grandfather of the two men, was said to be prostrate with grief. A private train took the survivors, Mrs. Widener and her maid, to Philadelphia.

Mrs. Ryerson had already lost a son, and now she had lost her husband. According to the *New York Times,* she was said to have suffered a serious nervous breakdown.

Edith Candee Mathews, Helen Churchill Candee's daughter, was waiting anxiously on the pier that night. Edith had had no word from her mother, none of the "am safe" messages heard up and down the Maine coast as *Carpathia* neared land. Mrs. Candee's name had been misspelled on the passenger list. She had been traveling alone, and had the worry of her son on her mind. Had she survived? The realization that all women had not been saved had been obvious from comparing the passenger list and the survivor list.

After docking, Candee waited in her cabin for a while, allowing the crowd to lessen to make it easier for her to disembark with her injured ankle. This only caused increased concern for her daughter. Edith's eyes scanned the disembarking passengers, and when she saw her mother, being carried like a baby because of her injury, Edith started waving her arms and laughing hysterically. Mrs. Candee was whisked away to stay with the Mathews family on 57th Street, turning down offers of assistance from the Relief Committee.

On April 19, the *New York Journal* would identify William Sloper as the man who had survived the *Titanic* sinking dressed as a woman.

As *Carpathia* came into dock, Sloper could make out the face of newspaper editor William Gleason, standing next to his father and older brother. Gleason asked Sloper if he had a story for him, and Sloper told him to come to the Waldorf-Astoria for it.

After leaving *Carpathia,* Sloper, his father, and his brother Harold took a taxicab to the Waldorf-Astoria on Fifth Avenue, arriving there at 10:45 p.m. Though the area was deserted, as soon as Sloper registered at the desk, he was surrounded by about two hundred people, asking him questions about what had happened. Not having eaten since two p.m. (partly because *Carpathia* was running low on food), a room service order was placed, and shortly thereafter the editors of the *Hartford Times* and the *New Britain Herald* arrived.

Sloper produced his handwritten story, and the two men left immediately to have it typed up by a stenographer. As Sloper's brother Harold tried to close their hotel room door, he was confronted by about fifteen or twenty other newspapermen, all looking for a story. Harold told them he would check with his brother to see if he wanted to talk to them, and abruptly shut the door in their faces. Sloper's father advised his son not to talk to them, saying they would distort his words and scoop the Connecticut papers.

"When my brother reopened the door in order to give our decision to the waiting reporters, they tried again to crowd into my room," recounted Sloper. "In order to prevent them, my brother had to throw his weight against the ones in front, forcing them back into the hall before closing the door again in their faces."

This incident led to a reporter from the *New York Journal* writing "a nasty paragraph about [Sloper] which appeared on the front page of his morning newspaper." According to the *Journal,* "William T. Sloper, son of prominent Connecticut banker, was rescued from the *Titanic* disguised in a woman's nightgown."

Frederic Spedden had been part of the survivors' committee, formed on *Carpathia*. Upon arrival in New York, they delivered the following statement:

> We, the undersigned surviving passengers from the SS *Titanic*, in order to forestall any sensational or exaggerated statements, deem it our duty to give to the press a statement of facts which have come to our knowledge and which we believe to be true.
>
> On Sunday, April 14, 1912, at about 11:40 p.m., on a cold starlit night in a smooth sea and with no moon, the ship struck an iceberg which had been reported to the bridge by lookouts, but not early enough to avoid collision. Steps were taken to ascertain the damage and save passengers and ship. Orders were given to put on life belts and the boats were lowered. The ship sank at about 2:30 a.m. Monday, and the usual distress signals were sent out by wireless and rockets fired at intervals from the ship. Fortunately the wireless messages were received by the Cunard SS *Carpathia* at about 12 o'clock midnight, and then she arrived on the scene of the disaster at about four a.m. Monday.
>
> The officers and crew of the SS *Carpathia* had been preparing all night for the rescue and comfort of the survivors, and the last mentioned was received on board with the most touching care and kindness, every attention being given to all irrespective of class. The passengers, officers, and crew gave up gladly their staterooms, clothing, and comforts for our benefit, all honor to them . . .
>
> We feel it our duty to call the attention of the public to what we consider the inadequate supply of lifesaving appliances provided for on modern passenger steamships and recommend that immediate steps be taken to compel passenger steamers to carry sufficient boats to accommodate the maximum number of passengers carried on board. The following facts were observed and should be considered in this connection.
>
> The insufficiency of lifeboats, rafts, etc.; lack of trained seamen to man same (stokers, stewards, etc. are not efficient boat handlers); not enough officers to carry out emergency orders

from the bridge and superintend the launching and control of lifeboats, absence of searchlights.

The board of trade rules allow for entirely too many people in each boat to permit the same to be properly handled. On the *Titanic,* the boat deck was about 75 feet above water, and consequently, the passengers were requested to embark before lowering boats, thus endangering the operation and preventing the taking on of the maximum number the boats would hold. Boats at all times to be properly equipped with provisions, water, lamps, compasses, lights, etc. Lifesaving boat drills should be more frequent and thoroughly carried out; and officers should be armed at boat drills. Greater reduction in speed in fog and ice, as damage if collision actually occurs is liable to be less.

In conclusion, we suggest that an international conference be called to recommend the passage of identical laws providing for the safety of all at sea, and we urge the US government to take the initiative as soon as possible.

The coming-out party for J. P. Morgan's granddaughter, Jane Morgan, in New York was canceled, as were the festivities for Morgan's birthday party, which fell on April 17, two days after *Titanic* sank. Morgan was described by his son-in-law as entirely absorbed by the news of the sinking. He had been scheduled to sail on that voyage, and many of his friends were on board; in addition, the captain and ship's officers were all old shipmates of his. He was also deeply hurt by news reports that his company had put money ahead of safety.

On Thursday, the White Star Line offices sent a telegram to Joseph M. White, Percival Sr.'s oldest brother, saying there was no probable chance that he was among the saved. Joseph White and his brother, John, went to New York to await the arrival of the *Carpathia* anyway, while Edith traveled to Boston to be with her other son, Percival Jr.

Joseph and John waited in the baggage claim area, in Section W, under the initial of the last name of the desired passenger. They waited until all of the 720 survivors had disembarked, questioning many survivors as they left the ship. The brothers got few, if any, answers.

"The arrival of the *Carpathia* in New York brought no news in regard to Percival W. White and Richard F. White of this town, who were passengers on the *Titanic,* and there can be no doubt that they lost their lives in the disaster to that ship," wrote one Brunswick newspaper.

There was no information for the Whites at all. There were no wives to whom the men had bid good-bye who could tell the tale of their last minutes. They were not well-known like the Astors, so were not the object of constant observation. The White family found no consolation at the pier . . . so they decided to get information on their own.

Maine's newspapers summed up the state's—and the country's—feelings on the sinking of the *Titanic.*

"Suspense is ended at last, and the world knows the salient facts of the catastrophe to the gigantic White Star liner. Much of the detail is yet to be untangled from the varying statements of survivors, but on the main features there is a general consensus of testimony. It is a thrilling story packed with heartrending incidents, with hair's-breadth escapes, with deeds of self-sacrifices and heroism, with graphic details of the suffering of the survivors and of the fate of the man, the few exceptions to the rule, who sought to disregard the order of 'Women and children first,' " wrote the daily *Eastern Argus.*

"Was there ever such a pitiful, agonizing homecoming as that of the survivors on the *Carpathia?*," wrote the weekly *Eastern Argus.* "The thought of the human misery and suffering of it all staggers the imagination and hardens the heart of the whole civilized world."

"Not all the tears are shed by the survivors and the relatives of those who perished. The whole world weeps in this common sorrow," the *Portland Evening Express* wrote. "No doubt there were among those hundreds men who did not know how to live, but it must forever remain in the minds of all that they knew how to die."

The *Republican Journal* of Belfast wrote: "Details are not needed to impress upon the mind the magnitude of this horror, the unspeakable sorrow and suffering it has caused." And the *Portland Evening Express* noted, "If it was a record the *Titanic* was after, she made it! The horror was fully as great as had been feared."

Sunday, three days after *Carpathia* had arrived in port, the pulpits of churches all over Maine were turned over to what lessons could be learned from the *Titanic* disaster.

In Waterville, Reverend E. C. Whittemore, pastor of the First Baptist Church, chose the topic "For the Sake of Others," mentioning the heroism of the men aboard *Titanic* in staying behind for the sake of saving the lives of the women aboard.

Congregational Church Reverend C. F. Stimson preached on the subject of "The Race is Not to the Swift," referencing Ecclesiastes. "The sinking of the *Titanic* with over 1,500 persons on board," said Reverend Stimson, "reveals the criminal cost of unmoralized commercialism, defeating both science and civilization."

In Portland, at the Free Street Sunday School, Superintendent H. Wallace Noyes asked the members of the school to unite in silent prayer for the survivors, during which the school's orchestra played Chopin's Funeral March.

At the First Free Baptist Church in Portland, Reverend Albert W. Jefferson gave his sermon, at the end of which the choir sang "Nearer, My God, To Thee." Jefferson's sermon was a tribute to the unselfish spirit shown by those on *Titanic* who gave their lives so others could get in the lifeboats. At the church, the Union Jack and the Stars and Stripes were draped together.

In Bath, the People's Church held a special memorial service to honor those lost on the *Titanic*. The service included special music by a choir and a quartet, and a violinist, Professor Stevens. The title of the minister's sermon was "The Tragedy."

In the Lewiston/Auburn area, a memorial service was held at the Free Baptist Church on Court Street. The entire congregation stood and offered a silent prayer for those lost in the disaster. Reverend A. J. Marsh would preach on the subject in the evening.

Reverend G. E. Kinney of the Sixth Street Congregational Church in Auburn preached to his flock: "Men are of more value than machines, mills, factories, buildings, bridges, mines, railways, or steamships. The needless loss of life in our modern industries is appalling."

Reverend J. F. Clothey of the Turner Street Advent Church in Auburn said, "The greatest lesson from the *Titanic* disaster is the necessity of being prepared for death. None of us knows how soon we may be called from the world. For this reason we should be prepared for eternal life. Those who already have not given their souls to Christ should do so, for they know not what the morrow may bring forth."

Reverend C. H. Temple of the First Universalist Church of Lewiston said: "Grief knits us together with the common bond of brotherhood as nothing else can do."

The *Laurentic* of the White Star Dominion Line and the *Ausonia* of the Cunard Line came into Portland on April 22, 1912, four days after *Carpathia* had arrived. Commander J. Mathias, Lieutenant, RNR, of the steamship *Laurentic,* was well-known in Portland, where he had a great many friends. In 1896 he had come to the city as fourth officer of the Dominion liner *Vancouver,* returning every year until 1901. He had served as first officer of the *Cambroman,* and he was chief officer of the *Columbus,* later renamed the *Republic.* His first command was in 1904, taking charge of the steamer *Victorian* of the White Star Line. He assumed command of the *Laurentic* a year before *Titanic* sank.

Laurentic and *Ausonia* arrived in Portland within ten minutes of each other. The *Ausonia* had left Southampton one day after *Titanic.* The seven hundred passengers of the *Laurentic* were not made aware of the *Titanic* disaster until they had arrived in Halifax on Saturday, April 20, and the 985 passengers and crew of *Ausonia* did not know of the disaster until they arrived in Portland. Commander Mathias and the wireless operator were the only two men aboard the *Laurentic* who knew about *Titanic's* sinking, keeping the news from the passengers and officers of the ship.

The passengers of another ship that arrived in Portland, the *Cymric,* did not know about the sinking until they arrived in Portland on the morning of April 19, with 1,080 passengers on board, as well as freight.

One of those passengers was Dr. J. M. Edwards, a prominent physician from Mankato, Minnesota. He and his wife had planned to sail on *Titanic,* but were delayed in Wales, so sailed to Portland on the *Cymric.* He and some of the other passengers said they had felt the cold when they were in the vicinity of the icebergs off the Grand Banks. Dr. Edwards provided the *Portland Evening Express* with pictures of the icebergs they had passed, which the paper printed.

"I believe [our captain] was wise in not giving us news of the terrible disaster," said Dr. Edwards. "If he had given the passengers information regarding the *Titanic* when he received the first wireless dispatch, the greater number of passengers on board the *Cymric* would never have left the decks of our steamer. I am thankful that I did not learn the news until the *Cymric* arrived in Portland."

Another ship's captain who was well-known in Portland was James Henry Moore of the Canadian Pacific Railroad steamship, *Mount Temple*. Captain Moore had come to Portland as commander of the *Cambroman* of the old Dominion Line, and was later charged by his passengers with having been within five miles of *Titanic*'s sinking.

Passenger E. W. Zurich had crossed from Antwerp to St. John, New Brunswick, on the *Mount Temple*, which carried two thousand people. He made a statement concerning what was observed from the *Mount Temple* at sea on the Sunday night the *Titanic* went down. According to Zurich, passengers on the *Mount Temple* were made aware of the *Titanic*'s distress at 12:15 a.m. on Monday when a wireless call for help was heard by the ship. According to Zurich, Captain Moore changed his vessel's course and headed for the *Titanic*. Lifeboats were swung from davits and other preparations were made in order to lend assistance to the stricken liner. Zurich said the new course was not held for long, however, because of the ice. Zurich heard through other passengers and crew that no further attempts were made to help the *Titanic*.

Dr. F. C. Quitzrau testified before the US Senate shortly after the sinking. He was traveling in Second Class aboard the *Mount Temple*, which left Antwerp on April 3, 1912. He said he was awakened about midnight on Sunday, New York time, by the sudden stopping of engines. He immediately went to the deck, where several stewards and passengers had already gathered. They informed him that word had been received by wireless from the *Titanic* that they had struck an iceberg and were calling for help. Quitzrau's testimony continued:

> Orders were immediately given and the *Mount Temple* course changed, heading straight for the *Titanic.* About three o'clock New York time (two o'clock ship's time), the *Titanic* was sighted by some of the officers and crew . . . as soon as the *Titanic* was seen, all lights on the *Mount Temple* were put out and the engines stopped. [T]he boat lay dead for about two hours.
>
> [A]s soon as day broke, the engines were started and the *Mount Temple* circled the *Titanic*'s position, the officers insisting that this be done, although the captain had given orders that the boat proceed on its journey. While encircling the *Titanic*'s position we sighted the *Frankfurt* to the northwest of us, the *Birma* to the south; speaking to both of these by wireless, the latter asking if we were in distress.
>
> [A]t about six o'clock we saw the *Carpathia,* from which we had previously received a message that the *Titanic* had gone down; at about 8:30 the *Carpathia* wirelessed that it had picked up 20 lifeboats and about 720 passengers all told, and that there was no need for the *Mount Temple* to stand by, as the remainder of those on board were drowned.

Captain Moore said he was awakened by a steward at 12:30 on Monday morning with a Marconi message from *Titanic,* requesting assistance. According to Moore, he immediately blew the whistle on the bridge once and changed course, steering for *Titanic.* He ordered his officers to give the firemen a tot of rum to get the ship moving faster.

While making for *Titanic,* Captain Moore said that in the darkness, they encountered an ice pack, estimating it to be five to six miles wide, extending north and south beyond what you could see with the naked eye. Moore said that he saw forty or fifty icebergs, with one being two hundred feet above the waterline. At 3:25 a.m. ship's time they stopped, then proceeded slowly, estimating that they were about fourteen miles from *Titanic*'s position. Moore told of seeing a tramp steamer with a light.

Moore denied reports that they had seen *Titanic*'s rockets. He said no passengers were on deck to his knowledge, and that his ship's stewards had also reported that no one was on deck. He made gangways and ladders ready for lowering, and ordered all officers on deck to try to spot anything they could. Captain Moore said they saw no wreckage or bodies—nothing. He looked for a thin spot to go through the ice, but could find none. He reminded the Senate committee that his company had standing orders not to enter an ice pack.

"I assure you that I did everything that was possible, sir," Moore told Senator William Alden Smith during the Senate's inquiry into the sinking, "consistent with the safety of my own ship and its passengers." Smith complimented Moore on his safe handling of his ship.

"I shall believe Captain Moore's story of the matter," said Captain Mathias of the *Laurentic,* who had served with Captain Moore. "I do not believe that he was within five miles of the *Titanic* and that the passengers on the *Mount Temple* saw the *Titanic* go down. Captain Moore was a very efficient officer, and I believe that the charges against him will prove untrue when the investigation is completed."

Shortly after *Carpathia* had returned the survivors to New York, hearings began into the disaster. One member of the committee was Senator George Perkins, formerly from Kennebunk, now a senator from California. After several missteps by Senator William Alden Smith, the head of the Senate committee investigating the disaster, the *Boston Globe* suggested that Senator Perkins should take charge of the investigation in an editorial noted by the *Biddeford Weekly Journal.* The head of the committee, the *Globe* suggested, was from Michigan, and thus unfamiliar with things such as watertight compartments, which Senator Smith had suggested might still hold survivors two miles under the sea.

Perkins was described as coming from a humble home in Kennebunkport. Born in 1839, he was sixty-two at the time of the sinking. At age thirteen he had left home and gone to sea as a sailor. He would return home at age fifteen, go to school for six more months, and then leave again for the sea, eventually ending up in San Francisco.

"Pending the senator's further education, why would it not be a good plan for the committee to employ the services of a marine expert of some kind as the conductor of its inquiry, or at least turn the work over to that old salt, Senator Perkins of California, but sometimes of Kennebunk."

Perkins would later introduce a bill to the Senate requiring that ocean liners all carry sufficient lifeboats to accommodate every passenger on board.

After the Senate investigation was completed, the May 3, 1912, edition of the *Portland Evening Express* ran an editorial: "J. Bruce Ismay is on his way back to England. He says he has no ill feelings against the American public. Judging from the attitude of some of our citizens, however, we fear the sentiment is not absolutely reciprocal."

The local papers received praise for their coverage of the sinking and *Carpathia*'s arrival in New York: "To the Editor of the *Express-Advertiser:* It is only your due that I should say that in no newspaper, and I have seen them all, printed in the Eastern cities, is the news of the arrival of the *Carpathia,* and the details of the wreck of the *Titanic,* told with so much clearness, the matter so well arranged, or as interestingly told as it was in our issue of April 19. This is a free boost for the *Express-Advertiser.* A.S.B., Portland, April 20, 1912."

On April 20, Lyman W. Hanson of Portland wrote, "The readers of your paper will long remember the sacrifice you made to give us all the news concerning the arrival of the *Carpathia,* and the true story of the wreck of the *Titanic,* promptly."

On April 19, William T. Johnson—who said he was a stranger to Portland, having gone there from New York—wrote to the paper, saying he thought he would have had to wait for larger papers to get full coverage of the disaster. "A boy came to the hotel where I was stopping, offering the *Express-Advertiser* for sale. Thinking I would like to know what kind of an idea the newspaper men 'down east' had of this great story, and what they thought 'all about the wreck' meant, I purchased a paper. Imagine my astonishment when I unfolded the paper to see a 'layout' second to nothing that the great papers could offer. The story was handled with a skill that would have done credit to our most pretentious journals. I congratulate you."

The April 20 edition of the *Eastern Argus* featured the headline LITTLE LEFT TO TELL AFTER THE COMPLETE STORY IN YESTERDAY'S ISSUE.

X

All eyes now turned to Halifax, Nova Scotia, Canada.

The day before *Carpathia* arrived in the United States with *Titanic*'s survivors, a small cable repair ship called the *Mackay-Bennett* was leaving Halifax shortly after noon to gather *Titanic*'s dead. The ship had asked all other ships in the area to report if they passed wreckage or bodies.

On Saturday, April 22, they received word from the German mail boat SS *Rhein* that in latitude 42.01 north, longitude 49.13 west, they had passed both wreckage and bodies. The SS *Bremen* reported passing three large icebergs and some bodies in latitude 42.00 north, longitude 49.20 west.

Bad weather and fog detained the *Mackay-Bennett,* which meant the ship didn't arrive at the site of the wreck until Saturday, April 21. Bodies were found floating in groups, sometimes fifty or more, none lashed together. All bodies recovered were standing upright in the water. Some bodies were clad in pajamas, two and three shirts, two pairs of pants, two vests, two jackets, and an overcoat. In some pockets a quantity of meat and biscuits were found, while the pockets of most of the crew members contained quite a lot of tobacco and matches, along with keys to the various lockers and stateroom doors.

There were doors, chairs, and wood from the ship spread throughout the area. An empty, upside-down, flat-bottomed lifeboat was found with no bodies near it. They saw no signs of bullet wounds on any of the bodies. Several men were dressed in evening clothes.

Small boats with a crew of five men each were lowered by the *Mackay-Bennett* whenever a group of bodies was sighted, and into these craft were piled the dead, three or four at a time. During the night and the next day, the *Mackay-Bennett* covered an area of thirty square miles. Fifty-five bodies were recovered, twenty-four of them being recommitted to the sea. Hauled on board the cable repair ship, each body was numbered with a large canvas tag, and the valuables and papers found with each body were placed in a similarly numbered canvas sack.

According to the report of Captain F. H. Lardner, master of the *Mackay-Bennett,* the bodies bore indication that the victims had died swiftly, if not almost painlessly. Lardner stated: "In many cases their features were calm, and, with the exception of those who had been severely injured by debris while fighting for their lives in the disintegrating ship, they were remarkably free from the stamp of horror or suffering. All were in a remarkable state of preservation, for they had been found in the cold water north of the Gulf Stream."

John Snow Jr., the undertaker who was in charge of embalming the dead aboard the *Mackay-Bennett,* told a different story. Snow described the bodies as being mutilated, with shattered arms and legs and mangled faces and bodies. "There was awful evidence of the fierce struggle for life, hands clutching wildly at clothing, faces distorted with terror. But it is no use to try to describe what we saw. To do so is impossible. As I said, ours was a sickening task," said Snow. He added that all watches worn by the men had stopped at precisely ten minutes past two, to the second. "There was not the very slightest deviation," said Snow.

Snow told of a two-year-old boy whose body came floating to the *Mackay-Bennett,* his face upturned, wearing no life belt. "Nothing I saw at sea made such an impression upon me," said Snow.

By April 24, 205 bodies had been picked up by the *Mackay-Bennett.* Many of the bodies were buried at sea. One body was thought to be that of Mr. Widener, but later was believed to be his valet. The body was badly damaged, and was ultimately buried at sea. Lardner believed that all of the bodies buried at sea were members of the ship's company, and most of them were in such condition that they could not possibly have been brought ashore.

"It is my opinion that the bulk of the bodies are in the [*Titanic*]," said Captain Lardner. "I think when she went down, the water would [have broken] into her with great force and [driven] them into the hull. All the watches were stopped between 2 and 2:20 o'clock. I don't think there was a First Class woman passenger's body found. Mrs. Strauss's body was not found."

Lardner continued: "We buried so many at sea simply because we could not accommodate them. We had limited embalming supplies, and it was absolutely necessary to consign many to the deep. None, if any, passengers, I believe, were buried [at sea], except perhaps in the case of Mr. Widener's valet. The great majority of those sunk were unidentified without even clothing as a means to tell who they were. We had instructions when we left here to pick up all the *Titanic*'s dead we could. Under the conditions it was impossible to carry out those instructions.

"None of those whom we found it necessary to bury [at sea] were men of prominence," said Lardner.

Services were held on board the *Mackay-Bennett* for those buried at sea. The ship's bell was tolled to indicate all was in readiness for the service. Standing on the bow of the ship, as she rocked to and fro, one gazed at the starry heavens and across the boundless deep, and to his mind the Psalmist's words came with mighty force: "Whither shall I go then from Thy Spirit, or whither shall I go then from Thy presence; if I ascend up to heaven Thou art there; if I make my bed in the grave, Thou are there also; if I take the wings of the morning and dwell in the uttermost part of the sea, even there shall Thy hand lead me, and Thy right hand shall hold me," recited Reverend Canon Hind.

In the solemn stillness of the early night the words of that unequaled burial service rang out across the waters: "I am the resurrection and the life, saith the Lord; he that believeth in Me, though he were dead, yet shall he live, and whosoever liveth and believeth in Me shall never die." The words were spoken over each body: "For as much as it hath pleased Almighty God to take unto Himself the souls of our dear brother departed, we therefore commit his body to the deep to be turned to corruption, looking for the resurrection of the body (when the sea shall give up her dead) and the life of the world to come through Jesus Christ our Lord, who shall change our vile body, that it may be like unto His glorious body, according to the mighty working whereby He is able to subdue all things to Himself."

Prayers from the burial service were spoken, the hymn "Jesus, Lover of my Soul" was sung, and the blessing was given. "It is to be noted how earnestly and reverently all the work was done, and how nobly the crew acquitted themselves during [the] work of several days, which meant a hard and trying strain on mind and body," said Hind. Three separate services were held for those recommitted to the sea, all performed by Canon K. O. Hind of Halifax's All Saint's Cathedral.

At midnight on April 25, the *Minia* arrived alongside the *Mackay-Bennett*.

Hays's body was found by the *Minia* at six a.m. on April 26. That same day, Astor's body was recovered by the *Mackay-Bennett*. The name of a recovered body listed as F. F. White also came through on a telegram from the *Mackay-Bennett* to the White Star Line, believed to be that of Richard White.

"Melancholy enough, the satisfaction of relatives in recovering the remains of *Titanic* victims," wrote one Maine newspaper.

Upon the announcement of the discovery of Richard White's body, a memorial service was planned for him at Bowdoin. The college's student-run publication, *The Bowdoin Orient,* paid tribute to Richard: *"The Orient* joins the whole community in lamenting the early death of a brilliant student, a popular and loyal undergraduate, and a true son of Bowdoin."

Delta Kappa Epsilon passed a resolution: "To his mother and brother, the Chapter extends its heartfelt sympathy in their double loss. To us he was a loved and honored brother, and we mourn his loss with them."

About a hundred people had arrived in Halifax to claim the bodies of those lost in the sinking. The list of passengers and the claimants included:

> Colonel Astor—Captain Roberts, Halifax Hotel
> Colonel Astor—Vincent Astor
> Colonel Astor—T. Hyde
> Mr. Thayer—Mr. Richardson, Halifax Hotel
> Mr. Hays—H. G. Kelley, Halifax Hotel
> Mr. Hays—Dr. Hutchinson
> Mr. Davidson—H. W. Brainerd
> Mr. Davidson—D. D. Hall
> Thornton Davidson—F. L. Davidson
> William M. Widener, G. O. Widener, M. Chase, G. O. Widener—car Constitution

The hotels were crowded with claimants, and each new train brought more. City windows showed markings of sympathy.

Those in Halifax to identify the bodies of their loved ones expressed great dissatisfaction at what they considered incomplete arrangements for their convenience and for the speedy dispatch of their sorrowful business. They said that the police arrangements to prevent crowding when bodies were taken from the dockyard were not what they should have been; that it was impossible to obtain information as promptly as it should have been provided; and that there should have been provisions made for nurses and doctors to be present at the dockyard, in case of illness or collapse of people shocked at the appearance of the dead who would be brought in, or in case family members collapsed because the bodies of their dead were *not* numbered among those recovered.

In response, Halifax officials organized a volunteer committee to try and remedy their concerns. They founded an informal bureau of information at the Halifax Hotel, where all inquiries would be responded to. The White Star Line kept a registry of all friends and relatives of *Titanic* victims who called.

Arrangements had been made with railroad companies to ship the bodies to any part of Canada or the United States as soon as possible after their identification. All formalities of crossing the border were waived. Unidentified bodies would be buried in the cemeteries of the denominations they belonged to, as well as could be ascertained. A full description of those who were as yet unidentified would be forwarded to the White Star Line offices in New York. Staff at these offices intended to publish this list in newspapers throughout the United States and Canada. "If a body is claimed after burial," officials announced, "the mayor of Halifax has promised to have it exhumed and shipped to relatives."

On April 29, at 9:40 a.m., the Canadian cable repair ship, *Mackay-Bennett,* with 190 bodies aboard—130 identified, 60 unidentified—arrived in port in Halifax with all the bodies she could handle. She was called the funeral ship. As soon as the ship was sighted, special canvas curtains were lowered at the shipyard. The

Mackay-Bennett would dock at Pier Number 4, the largest landing place, normally the home of the HMCS *Niobe,* which was in dry dock for repairs. Flags would be placed at half-mast, and church bells tolled.

The ship's afterdeck was piled high with coffins, her forward hold piled with unshrouded bodies. The bodies were transferred silently and rapidly to a squad of undertakers, equipped with horse-drawn carriages. Sentries at the gates of the pier saluted every coffin. The police squad that joined the ship at quarantine looked as if they had been aboard for days.

About two hundred people gathered outside the pier. They all stood in silence, overlooking a terrace into the navy dockyard located six hundred yards away. They saw nothing but the upper structure of the *Mackay-Bennett.* Tents housed the coffins, and canvas covered the lane on which the dead were being ferried to the long file of undertakers' wagons, which wound their way up the hill to the morgue. A squad of twelve drilled men, members of the Dominion police force, were brought in from Ottawa, half of them for duty at the gates, the other half for the waterfront.

The bodies had been well-preserved when found in the water, but they became discolored while lying on the deck of the *Mackay-Bennett.* The bodies on the forward deck—the unidentified— were removed first. Colonel Astor's body was in one of the many coffins located on the ship's stern. Only a half-dozen claimants were at the pier, laced with empty coffins; the rest waited at the morgue.

Wagons removed the bodies from the navy yards and transported them to the improvised morgue located at the city's skating rink (also used for the popular Canadian sport of curling). Sailors worked for hours unloading the tragic cargo. By the time the first hearse arrived, the rink's spectator area was full of people. The looks on the claimants' faces were those of sorrowful expectation and dread.

"The scene at the Mayflower curling rink yesterday morning was one that will long be remembered. Never before in the history of Halifax had a charnel house been fitted for the accommodation of so many bodies; never before had so many bereaved ones assembled at a Halifax morgue from so many different places, yet all bent on the same errand—the hope of discovering a lost relative or friend," said a Halifax newspaper.

Outside, in front of the rink, a large crowd of men, women, and children gathered, watching the long rows of hearses as they arrived, unloaded, and came out again, returning for another load. People vied with each other for advantageous positions, and looked in all the windows of the rink. Photographers took pictures of the scene.

Inside the curling rink, behind a wooden partition, were thirty-four benches where embalmers did their work. As soon as a body was embalmed, it was taken to the main portion of the rink. The claimants occupied a raised platform overlooking the coffins.

An improvised hospital had been created in a space next to the waiting room by curtaining off one of the large dressing rooms. "This [area] was made all ready for the reception of those who had come for the purpose of identifying dear, lost relatives and friends, and who might well be expected to fall [into] a state of collapse when they recognized among the long rows of still and senseless forms those whom they had last seen in the full vigor of life and happiness," said the *Halifax Herald.*

A number of beds were there, with the whitest of linen, separated by screens. Everything was overseen by Miss Nellie Remby, an extremely compassionate nurse who was ready to render assistance at a moment's notice. In addition to the beds, restoratives were on hand. In another room there was a long table bountifully supplied with writing material of all kinds. The coroner's office was upstairs, where numerous staff members were engaged in doing their part.

"Never was a coroner's office more busy; never in the whole history of Halifax had it been called upon to adjudicate upon so many cases at one time," said the *Halifax Herald.*

A hush fell upon all in attendance as the first hearse unloaded its cargo: a rough coffin, which was put on one of the many white benches behind the partition. One by one the coffins were gently laid on the benches—some in the main part of the rink, some in the embalming room, which was segregated by curtains.

Strangers conversed with those near them as freely as if there was no such thing as conventionality. A common grief had broken down the cold barrier of society's caste system, and the thoughts and words of all were bent on the affliction which was weighing down the hearts of the claimants. "All were, for the time being, brothers in distress."

At first, while the coffins were unloaded, the claimants were allowed into the main part of the rink, but they were later asked to step aside until all had been unloaded. There, they could watch at a distance. Many paced around the room, impatient at the delay yet dreading to see that which they hoped might reveal the identity of a loved one. Every once in a while one of the claimants would say, "I must have fresh air," and they would go out into the bright sunlight for a few minutes, sometimes accompanied by a friend.

As fast as the bodies were embalmed they were taken into the inspecting room. The work took the entire day. At about four p.m. a semblance of order was achieved at the curling rink. The identified bodies were removed by undertakers and taken at once to the railway station or some private place in the city, where they were prepared for shipment to their final destination.

Colonel Astor's body was taken off the ship shortly before noon and brought with the others to the morgue. Captain Richard Roberts, commander of the Astor yacht, was the first to view

Astor's body. He said there was not the slightest doubt it was Colonel Astor. The body was clothed only in undergarments; his outer clothing and personal effects had been laid aside and tagged.

Vincent Astor had left New York in his private railroad car, the *Oceanic,* immediately after learning that his father's body had been recovered. Two other private cars were also attached to the regular New York to Portland train. Vincent arrived at Portland's Union Station at 8:30 a.m. His car was held on a side track until the Number 29 train from Boston arrived at 10:50 a.m. *Oceanic* and his other two private cars were attached to the rear of that train, and departed at 10:57 a.m.

Vincent did not go to the morgue or dockyard; instead, he stayed very close to his car in Halifax, avoiding all forms of publicity. Rumors circulated that special favors had been sought and granted to Vincent Astor, although they were denied by a city official.

Colonel Astor's body was taken to the *Oceanic,* where Vincent would have his first chance to view it. The body was well-preserved and showed no signs of mutilation or decomposition. Astor's body was sent back home with Vincent, while Captain Roberts remained in Halifax in hopes of identifying Astor's valet.

Astor's body arrived in New York on May 2, accompanied by his son. Every flag in the village of Rhinebeck, New York, was at half-mast. A special train brought the funeral party from New York. Colonel Astor was buried two days later.

"The recovery of the body of Colonel Astor is pleasing news," wrote the *Bath Daily Times.* "Whatever may have been the merits or demerits of his previous career, the New Yorker died a hero."

Two days before Richard White's body was found, Frank Arthur Smith of Calais, a classmate of Richard's, and a fellow member of Bowdoin's Delta Kappa Epsilon fraternity, left for Halifax to meet the *Mackay-Bennett*. Percival Jr., Richard's older brother, just could not do it. He had his own grief, as well as a grieving mother to care for, among other family responsibilities.

The results of Richard White's last physical at Bowdoin, including body measurements, were forwarded to Halifax officials to help in the identification of his body. Richard's body was found on April 26. Zadock Long White, Richard's uncle, sent a telegram to Frank Smith in Halifax that day: "Richard's body reported found; better return with it at once. Will meet you in Portland. See White Star officials for everything necessary. Look sharp for my brother's body. Wire me fully as soon as you can." Two days later Zadock would wire Smith $75 for expenses.

On Richard's body were found keys, a matchbox, a gold watch, and a ring. When the crew of the *Mackay-Bennett* found his remains, they had estimated Richard's age at thirty-seven. He was just twenty-one.

After Smith had identified Richard's body, it was shipped by train immediately, arriving on the Provincial Express at the North Station in Portland at 8:30 a.m., on the same train as John Jacob Astor's body, which was on its way back to Massachusetts.

Smith did not find Percival Sr.'s body.

Edward Kent's brother-in-law, Harry K. White, went to Halifax to claim Kent's body, which had also been identified on the *Mackay-Bennett*. A telegram Kent's sister Nora sent her husband told him to look for the miniature Mrs. Candee had given him for safekeeping: "Edward wore a seal ring like yours—crest, stags; stone seal ring, small oval, both on little finger, probably marked; possibly lady's miniature . . . no distinguishing marks on body."

Kent was found wearing a dress suit and a gray coat. On his person was found Candee's silver flask, two gold signet rings, a gold watch, gold eyeglasses, a knife, two wallets containing $48.75

in currency, two cuff-link studs and one cuff link, and the gold-framed miniature of Mary Churchill Hungerford.

On April 23, in response to a plea from the Kent family for any information about their brother's last minutes aboard *Titanic*, Kent's sister Charlotte received a letter from Mrs. Candee's daughter. The Kent family immediately made arrangements to interview Mrs. Candee.

On May 15 the Kents sent Mrs. Candee her flask and miniature via American Express.

"The flask is badly out-of-shape but the lovely miniature is not, I think, permanently harmed. I am glad you are to have them both again," wrote the Kent family.

With all of the condolences they had received, the White family still needed answers to how Percival and Richard had spent their last minutes. Under the name of the cotton manufacturing firm, Nelson D. White & Sons, they sent a letter to *Titanic* survivors that included pictures of both Percival and Richard.

> Can you tell [us] anything about Percival W. White or his son Richard F. White, passengers on the *Titanic*? Pictures enclosed. Did they send any message to anyone? Did you see them after the ship struck the iceberg?
>
> Please reply,
> Respectfully,
> Nelson D. White & Sons

The Whites received many responses. They were just beginning to learn what had happened to Percival and Richard.

The *Minia* arrived in Halifax on May 6 at 1:45 a.m. Charles Hays's body was one of seventeen that this ship was able to recover. According to Francis Dyke, a crewman on the *Minia*, Hays's was the first body found by that ship, at five a.m. on Friday morning,

April 26. The crew had no trouble identifying him, as he was carrying a lot of papers, as well as a watch with his name engraved on it. One of the documents found on his body was a fire insurance policy, along with future plans for the Grand Trunk Railway's Pacific expansion. The Hays estate would receive $200,000 from a personal accident insurance policy after the sinking.

The Halifax Board of Trade sent a wreath to the car in which Mr. Hays's remains would proceed to Montreal. When Hays's body arrived in Montreal, representatives from every department of the Grand Trunk Railway system were at the station.

The Portland Board of Trade passed a resolution on Hays's death:

> In recognition of the deep debt of gratitude which the citizens of Portland owe to Charles M. Hays, we recur with civic pride to the citizens who had the foresight to see that a railroad to the great Northern country would afford quick and short transfer of grain to one of the most accessible and greatest harbors on the North Atlantic. This great enterprise languished although the City in its corporate capacity failed in supplying such facilities as seemed required, until that broadminded man, Charles M. Hays, came forward to manage the Grand Trunk [Railway]. He asked and obtained from the financial institutions of the City aid to build two large elevators on the waterfront, which, with its wharves, afforded unrivaled facilities for loading and unloading steamships of the largest capacity, within easy reach of the ocean. His genius and farsighted intelligence made the dreams of our Poor and Preble a reality, and placed our City in the front rank as an ocean seaport for the great granaries of the Northwest.
>
> We mourn his untimely taking off. We bear sad witness to his grand force of character, and our great loss. His bravery and unselfishness were grandly displayed in his last moments of life. We extend to his widow, family, and friends our heartfelt sympathy in their great bereavement.

On April 25 the Grand Trunk Railway held a special memorial for Charles Melville Hays. All work stopped for five minutes, from 11:30 to 11:35 a.m., at the Grand Trunk terminal in Portland, and other Grand Trunk facilities, in honor of Hays. The Portland offices of the railway were draped in bunting of purple and black.

On board the two ocean liners in port, the *Laurentic* and the *Ausonia,* crews paused in their work. An impressive service was held aboard the *Laurentic,* owned partially by the White Star Line. Three hundred men and officers were assembled on the upper deck. The men, in their work uniforms, joined in the singing of "Nearer, My God, to Thee," played by the ship's orchestra. The American flag was at half-mast, as were the flags on the flagpoles on top of the Grand Trunk grain elevator.

All of the officials and clerks of the Grand Trunk Railway remained in their offices for the five-minute silent tribute, all standing with heads bowed. No telephone rang, and the telegraph was silent.

XI

. . . the noble death of one of our number must bear fruit in
our lives.

—Frank Arthur Smith, Bowdoin Class of 1912

The *Titanic* disaster brought out the best—and the worst—in
people.

The *Portland Express-Advertiser* started receiving subscrip-
tions for the relief of the survivors of *Titanic,* headed by Louis N.
Kamber of the American Clothing Company of Portland, who
gave $25. Kamber said he wanted Portland to have some tangible
part in the extension of relief to the survivors.

To the *Express-Advertiser:*

Gentlemen: The people of Boston, New York, and other cities
are making up relief funds for the poor unfortunate people of
the *Titanic* disaster. Believing it to be a worthy cause, and also
that Portland should have a part in this, I am sending you a
check for $25 to start a relief fund in this City.

Very truly yours,
Louis N. Kamber

J. P. Morgan and Company donated $10,000 to the relief fund.

Businesses quickly started cashing in on the disaster. In the April 18 edition of the *Portland Evening Express,* the day *Carpathia* arrived, G. M. Barney, Portland's state agent for The Travelers Insurance Company, posted a large ad with the words *Titanic* passengers in boldface type: "A million dollars' accident insurance carried by the *Titanic* passengers in The Travelers Insurance Co.—losses which would bankrupt many accident companies—will be paid by The Travelers without effort or delay. Our Accident policies are unequaled for liberality and security. Moral: Insure in The Travelers."

Four days after the ship landed, the *Lewiston Daily Sun* would run an advertisement that looked like a news story, with the headline WOMEN ALL AT SEA:

> There are thousands of women today entirely at sea, so to speak, as far as their ailments are concerned. Many are suffering in silence rather than consult[ing] a physician, while many others have sought advice and taken medicines without help, and are literally discouraged. Such women should remember that Lydia E. Pinkham's Vegetable Compound may be relied upon to act promptly and thoroughly in such cases. It strengthens the nerves and muscles and restores the female system to a normal healthy condition.

Two days after that, more classified ads started appearing; for example, in the *Portland Evening Express,* an ad announced that the W. M. Prilay Post Card Company in Pittsfield was soliciting local agents to sell the upcoming book, *Sinking of the* Titanic *and other Great Sea Disasters,* a book derived largely from Senate testimony and newspaper articles.

Dr. Ed. E. Briry, an agent for the New York Life Insurance Company, would run an advertisement in the *Bath Daily Tribune* with the headline WOMEN AND CHILDREN FIRST.

At intervals in the history of the world, Fearful Disasters occur in which hundreds of lives are lost. These catastrophes have a sobering effect. They make the whole world stop and think. They set men face-to-face anew with the two great fundamentals—Life and Death. How noble appears the God-born instinct of protecting helpless women and children, even at the sacrifice of one's own life.

The New York Life [Insurance Company] will pay to the survivors many thousands of dollars provided for them by the loving foresight of the husbands and fathers—heroes all—who went to their doom with the lost *Titanic.*

"Women and children first" is an undercurrent of thought in the minds of a majority of Bath men, as shown by the large amount of sound life insurance carried for them.

There are still quite a number of men—men able to take out insurance, but who illustrate the rule followed on Chinese ships: Men first—Women and Children last.

On April 30, the day the *Mackay-Bennett* was bringing *Titanic*'s dead into Halifax Harbor, the A. H. Scott Company, manufacturers of custom shirts on 273 Middle Street in Portland, ran an ad headlined ON BOARD THE TITANIC in the *Portland Evening Express:*

On board the Titanic there were many cases of fine foreign shirting materials consigned to American merchants and manufacturers. In our shirt factory at 273 Middle Street, there are also many pieces of fine shirting of both foreign and domestic manufacture. Have your shirts made to order from these goods, and you will get the maximum of shirt satisfaction.

In the May 1 edition of the *Bath Daily Times* appeared an advertisement, looking much like a news story, for Swett & Co. drugstore in Bath: "The remarkable case of Mrs. J. Richard White has attracted much attention, as she was in bad health for a long while," reads the ad, which goes on to advertise Vinol, a tonic touted to build up health at the time.

In early May, three weeks after *Titanic* sank, the *Daily Kennebec Journal* ran an ad for the Select Roller Rink: TONIGHT MOVING PICTURES AND ROLLER SKATING—THE *TITANIC* PICTURES. A regular news item beside the ad read:

> Manager Murree offers the moving-picture lovers of this city a treat for Thursday, Friday, and Saturday, for in addition to the regular moving pictures, pictures will be shown of the *Titanic* disaster.
>
> These will be the first pictures of this disaster that have been offered to the Augusta public at the Rink, and undoubtedly the house will be packed, for everybody is interested in the disaster of which so much has been reported in the newspapers for the past few weeks. This is one of the greatest wrecks ever known in history, and over 1,600 lives were lost by the sinking of the ship. Everybody should see these pictures in order to realize how horrible the disaster really was.

The morning after arriving home from the *Carpathia,* Mrs. Astor arose at about ten a.m., feeling refreshed after a ten-hour sleep. By now Mrs. Astor was reported much improved by Dr. Reuel B. Kimball, who said she was out of danger, although she still remained in bed.

Vincent Astor and a few intimate friends visited and tried to keep her mind off the ordeal. Nevertheless, she continued to recount the event over and over, including how she had to help bail out the lifeboat. Mrs. Astor was described as being in a highly nervous condition, suffering from the shock of her experience. Dr. Kimball said that in spite of her nervousness, she should be allowed to talk freely of her experience with relatives and attendants, which was believed to be the best way to relieve her feelings.

Mrs. Astor spent the first few days after her return in her room. Soon the nervous condition which had caused her friends such concern on the night of her arrival had passed almost entirely away, and Dr. Kimball said he had not had to give her a single drop of medicine. For a period of time Mrs. Astor was expected to be called before the Senate inquiry, but that idea was later dropped.

On April 24 Mrs. Astor spent a busy day with callers, among them a Bishop Grier from her church, who remained for nearly an hour. After he left, a dressmaker arrived, and Mrs. Astor spent two hours picking out fabrics for some new dresses. Dr. Kimball said her condition was as good as could be expected, and that her health was improving every day. Two days later, when word was received that her husband's body had been found, Dr. Kimball and members of Mrs. Astor's family denied rumors that Madeleine had suffered a relapse and was critically ill.

"Mrs. Astor is still suffering from physical and nervous shock," said Dr. Kimball. "She is still in such a state that any reference to her horrible experience is to be avoided. But as to her actual state of health, she was better Tuesday than at any time since she reached New York." The doctor said he was no longer calling at the house every day, instead using the telephone to check on her condition. Dr. Kimball said the only thing that would prevent Mrs. Astor from going out for a drive would be the curiosity of people who might recognize her.

Within a few days of _Carpathia_'s arrival, speculation had already begun about the Astor will. Word was leaked to the press that the will would be probated in a few days, and that it was a new document, drawn up after Astor's marriage to Madeleine. The estate was estimated to be valued at $125 million. The reading of the will was postponed until Astor could be buried.

On May 6—two days after Astor's funeral—the Astor will was made public, although there was no formal reading. According to the legal document, Madeleine would receive $100,000 outright and $5 million in a trust, while her unborn child would receive a

$3 million trust. She would receive the town house and stable at the corner of Fifth Avenue and 65th Street, along with books, paintings, statues, other artwork, household effects, etc. She also got the horses and other livestock, and all equipment and supplies for the stable. Vincent essentially got the rest. If Madeleine were to remarry, however, her inheritance would all revert to Vincent. Bar Harbor cousin John F. Kane had served as a witness to the will's signing.

The will having been made public, the public's thoughts now turned to Mrs. Astor's social position. "Had Colonel Astor lived, it is probable that his bride eventually would have been accepted in his set as a leader," wrote one newspaper. "But as the colonel died before she could be established in that position, and as before her marriage she starred on tennis courts, rather than in ballrooms, it is considered doubtful whether she can ever become the social celebrity that she surely would have become had her husband lived."

After Astor's funeral, Madeleine took a daily drive or walk through Central Park. She spent a portion of each day with her mother or sister, and received no other callers. "The girl-widow, now looking forward to an early motherhood, has not expressed any desire for the visits of old-time friends. She lives secluded in the big mansion in Fifth Avenue," wrote one newspaper. Madeleine's father was looking after her financial interests, with the aid of competent counsel. Madeleine was keeping her future plans a secret, even within her own family.

On May 31, Captain Arthur Rostron of the *Carpathia* was a guest at a luncheon hosted by Mrs. Astor at her home on Fifth Avenue, to formally thank him for their rescue. Mrs. Thayer and fellow First Class passenger Mrs. John Bradley also attended. From there, Rostron went to Haverford, Pennsylvania, for a brief visit at Mrs. Thayer's home.

Also that month, the *New England Resorter*—a magazine devoted to news of all the New England summer colonies—announced that Mrs. John Jacob Astor would spend her summer in Bar Harbor. The story was quickly reprinted by the *Bar Harbor Record.*

It was also rumored that Mrs. Astor would wear white, not black, while in mourning for her late husband. The magazine reported that although Mrs. Astor herself thought it best to wear black, her mother believed she was too young to do that, worrying that the color might depress her spirits and affect her health, especially during her pregnancy. Gowns were ordered and made, cut along simple lines and only a touch stylish. Some were made of white crepe, her lounging robes being made of a fine silk. The clothing was made by a fashionable Fifth Avenue clothing store that specialized in mourning apparel.

The *Portland Evening Express* applauded the decision, and looked forward to the effect Mrs. Astor's decision would have on society: "If the usage of black can be changed, it will be a boon to humanity. Death is sad enough without making it more impressive and gloomy by the trapping and habiliments of woe. Less and less do we thrust our private troubles into public notice. All of us have troubles and griefs which we cannot betoken. Why should one particular sorrow be singled out for exhibition?"

Since Madeleine's due date was in August, her summer plans were later changed: She would stay in New York for the summer. Although Mrs. Astor had wanted to have her baby in the country, Vincent persuaded her to have it at the mansion, where he had been born. He believed it to be the proper place for the birth of an Astor heir.

Mrs. Astor's mother had been with her constantly since the *Titanic* disaster, along with her sister, Katherine. Newspapermen were standing watch outside the house, waiting for news of the birth, giving rise to a new institution, "the birth watch."

On August 14, 1912, John Jacob "Jakey" Astor VI was born. The birth was announced in a bulletin from Mrs. Astor's doctor: "Mrs. Astor has a son, born at 8:15 o'clock. His name is John Jacob Astor. Mother and son are in good condition."

The servants all wore broad smiles as they gave out the doctor's bulletin, and there was much excitement both within and outside the house. The baby was said to be strong, well-formed, and bearing a striking resemblance to his father. The newest Astor weighed seven pounds and three-quarters of an ounce.

Mr. Force visited the house shortly after the birth of his grandson. Mrs. Astor received many messages of congratulations from friends and relatives, including a cablegram from Vincent, who was on a motor trip on the European continent with his mother. Shortly after the cablegram was received, an immense box of American Beauty roses—Colonel Astor's favorite flower, and the type that he had often given his new bride—was sent to her from Vincent.

Margaret "Molly" Brown cabled her congratulations. In memory of the *Titanic* victims, and in honor of Madeleine, she sponsored a fund-raiser for a new maternity ward at the hospital in Newport, Rhode Island. One hundred Newport women pledged their sponsorship for this new ward.

The following summer, in 1913, Mrs. Astor did make her way back to Bar Harbor. She had arranged to stay at La Selva cottage, on Eden Street, and ordered that preparations be completed by June 1. Her servants arrived early in June with a baby perambulator (baby carriage). Mrs. Astor was to be accompanied by her son, John Jacob Astor, who was said to be developing into a vigorous boy, along with her sister, Katherine, and her mother. Because of her state of mourning, she was not expected to participate in social activities.

According to the *Bangor Daily News,* the press was anxious to get a picture of young John Jacob Astor, and had been making all efforts to obtain such, even as his family was making all efforts to prevent it. "The local newspapermen have been besieged with demands for the securing of such a photograph, and a news photographer from one of the large cities has been here for a week in a vain attempt to secure a snapshot of the features of the heir of the late John Jacob Astor," wrote the *Bangor Daily News.*

Madeleine's mother and sister partook in many of Bar Harbor's social events that season, but Madeleine did not. On July 30 Mrs. Force and Katherine attended a dinner at the Swimming Club, where one could expect to find morning concerts, noontime dancing, a cabaret tea every afternoon at five p.m., and moving pictures on Mondays and Thursdays. Supper dances were held on Tuesdays and Saturdays at ten p.m. Musicians from the Boston Symphony Orchestra played at the daily concerts. This was the year that the turkey trot was finally allowed at the Swimming Club, having been frowned upon before, along with the tango and other dances. There were also tennis tournaments, although Madeleine, tennis champion in days gone by, did not participate, as she stayed home with the baby.

"Mrs. John Jacob Astor still refuses to indulge in even the mildest social activities and wears heavy mourning clothes . . . ," reported the *Bar Harbor Record* at the end of the 1913 summer season.

Two days after Christmas that year, Mrs. Astor was present at the dedication of a memorial window at the Church of the Messiah in Rhinebeck, New York, along with her mother and sister, while her son remained in the city. Mrs. Astor wore a black dress trimmed with wide bands of black fox fur, a hat with a mourning veil, and a black fur coat. Her only jewelry was a large rope of pearls with a pendant. As she walked up the aisle, the church organist played "O, Come, All Ye Faithful."

The memorial window contained three panels, the central one depicting Christ walking on water. The memorial inscription read IN LOVING MEMORY OF JOHN JACOB ASTOR. BORN JULY 13, 1864. DIED APRIL 15, 1912.

The following year, in May 1914, Mrs. Astor took her son to Hot Springs, Virginia, for the health of the child. By June 17, Mrs. John Jacob Astor's domestics had arrived on Mount Desert Island, and the following month, Mrs. Astor was back at La Selva cottage on Eden Street, in Bar Harbor.

Now that two years had passed since Astor's death, Madeleine began to socialize more that summer. She went to the swimming pool with a guest, Helen Dodge of New York. On July 6 she participated in the ladies' golf tournament. A week later she and her sister were guests at a luncheon at the Malvern Hotel.

People who socialized with Madeleine that summer were struck by the wisdom that fell easily from her young lips. They found her quite able to carry on her end of a conversation on such subjects as ethics, biblical history, and even socialism. "Often she has been heard to remark 'as [Thomas] à Kempis says in his *The Imitation of Christ,*' or, 'Speaking of socialism, if you will read [James] Keir Hardie's *From Serfdom to Socialism,* you will see it in entirely a new light. I am sure I did,' " reported one local paper.

Such references from the widow of renowned capitalist Astor were just a bit startling to some of her more conservative friends, until they learned that she had picked up her education at the New York Training School for Deaconesses, and that she had gleaned her knowledge of socialism under the tutelage of Reverend Arthur Price Hunt, professor of Christian ethics at the General Theological Seminary.

Mrs. Astor was enrolled in the Training School for Deaconesses for the term that closed the first of May as a nonresident special student, confining her attention to Reverend Hunt's course in Christian ethics. The course featured a varied reading list, including John Peters's *Early Hebrew Story*, James Stalker's *The Ethics of Jesus*, Thomas à Kempis's *The Imitation of Christ*, William James's *The Varieties of Religious Experience*, Vida Dutton Scudder's *Socialism and Character*, Conrad Noel's *Socialism in Church History*, Walter Rauschenbusch's *Christianity and the Social Crisis*, Frederick Engels's *The Origin of the Family*, Olive Schreiner's *Woman and Labour*, and James Keir Hardie's *From Serfdom to Socialism.*

Mrs. Astor's aim was not to fit herself for active church work. According to a member of the school, she was induced to take Hunt's special course by Astor cousin Miss Sybil Kane of 23 West 47th Street, a close friend of Madeleine's and a special student at the school.

As had been the case after her engagement to Colonel Astor was announced, Madeleine was the center of Bar Harbor's attention during that summer of 1914. Barely a day went by without her participation in a tennis or golf tournament; in fact, she won many of the tennis competitions. Whenever Madeleine played, the lawn surrounding the tennis court was filled with spectators. It seemed that fashion's whirl might get ahold of her once again.

Vincent Astor was married on August 4 of that year, and he and his new bride sailed into port at Bar Harbor aboard his yacht, *Norma.* Astor boarded the SS *Kronprinzessin Cecilie* and interviewed the captain. He did not land in Bar Harbor, but sailed out again later that evening. It is not known whether he visited with Madeleine.

On August 19 it was announced that Mrs. John Jacob Astor had accepted a place on the women's peace parade committee in New York. She telegraphed her acceptance and her approval of the plan from Bar Harbor. A week later she was a patroness of the Red Cross Benefit Ball, which was called the event of the summer, if not the most interesting event ever held at Bar Harbor, both in a social and a patriotic way. Held at the Swimming Club, a supper was served in a huge tent behind the club building, keeping the whole of the clubhouse clear for dancing. There were many amusing and interesting novelties for sale as souvenirs, almost everything donated. The goal was to keep everyone's mind on the purpose of the ball: to support Red Cross work in Europe.

Mrs. Astor continued her socializing and athletic activities well into September, and stayed on the island through the end of October. It seemed she did not want to go home.

Bar Harbor society expected a big season in 1915, owing to the fact that people were unable to go abroad because of the war, which had broken out in August of 1914. Summer bookings were already coming in for the hotels as early as October 1914. The *New York Times* printed weekly news of the happenings at the resort area.

In April of 1915, Mrs. Astor visited Mrs. Widener, her fellow *Titanic* survivor, in Philadelphia. During that visit, the party traveled in a special car to Mount Vernon, and later visited the battlefield in Fredericksburg. As a result of the visit, the *New York Tribune* reported that there were rumors of a possible engagement between Clarence H. Mackay, president of the Postal Telegraph Company, and Mrs. John Jacob Astor.

Vincent Astor was asked about the rumor. "I haven't seen Mrs. Madeleine Force Astor for several weeks, so I cannot comment on this report," he said. "I do not know whether she is engaged to Mr. Mackay or not, nor do I know whether anything of that sort is probable. So far as I know they are merely friends."

Mrs. Astor was very busy in 1915. In May, young John Jacob Astor sat for a sculpture. The small statuette depicted a nude young Astor in an alert attitude, as if he were enjoying his freedom from clothes. The sculptor had a difficult time catching the active baby in the appropriate pose. Nonetheless, the finished product was described as a remarkably good likeness, full of beauty and grace, and was much admired by all.

Later in May, Madeleine Astor would be forced to fight her tax valuation in New York. On May 28, Mrs. Astor filed a report with the Surrogate's Court, reporting that she was spending more than $60,000 for the maintenance of the home on Fifth Avenue for herself and her son. She was allowed, under the office of the surrogate, to spend $20,000, the money coming out of the trust left by Colonel Astor.

Under the costs listed were one-third of the expenses of the Fifth Avenue mansion, taxes on the mansion, and fees for lawyers and doctors, among other things. Mrs. Astor reported spending $90,000 since her son's birth on employees, service, supplies, general upkeep, and other necessary household expenses. She spent $5,000 for clothes, supplies, toys, and other things for her baby since his birth. Mrs. Astor added that her legal counsel had advised her that he would give her more if necessary.

Mrs. Astor noted that she had not charged her son rent for his summer homes in Bar Harbor, nor the trips on which he had accompanied her. She reported that while she had received a little over $40,000 since his birth for his expenses, she had actually spent $64,000. "I have expended for the benefit of said infant, from the date of his birth to December 31, 1914, from my own resources—in addition to the amount received by me for his account—the sum of $23,600."

Mrs. Astor would later petition for an increase in her allowance for Baby Astor's upkeep, asking for $30,000 a year rather than $20,000.

On June 15, the *Waterville Sentinel* weighed in on the Baby Astor issue, which the *Bar Harbor Times* reprinted.

> Last year his toys cost $5,000, and everybody knows that as a boy gets bigger, the toys cost more. When the boy gets to be

six years old, what a hardship it would be if half his income were required to keep him in playthings.

The case of Baby Astor has been attracting much attention. There are many people who are indignant at the thought that his toys should cost so much. These good people have a great deal to say about the things which $5,000 would buy for children of the poor. But perhaps, the saddest figure in the story is that of the little one whose playthings cost thousands of dollars annually. He will never know a lot of fun that comes to other boys.

For with a $5,000 allowance for toys go a lot of other things. There are nurses and guardians who watch a little fellow every hour of the day. He never gets a chance to steal away and go in swimming with the other fellows. He will be taught to swim, of course, but he will never know the fun of cutting across back lots to dive into the big pool under the willows.

When the circus comes to town, he will go and sit in a box. But he won't have the exquisite delight of getting up in the early morning to see the trains come in and follow the wagons to the lot with, perhaps, the chance of actually carrying water for the elephants. And he will never know the pleasure of getting out with the other fellows and rollicking around until there are rents in his clothes and his face is plastered with the mud of Mother Earth.

He will be brought up by hard-and-fast rules administered by paid experts. He will be a machine-made product and, in some ways, will never have any boyhood. We do not regard this heir to the Astor millions as an object of envy.

On the other hand, those good folk who are freely predicting that he will be spoiled are indulging in a good deal of unnecessary anxiety. For he may grow into a good and capable man notwithstanding the handicap of $5,000 worth of toys and the other troubles which come to the children of the very rich.

Also in May it was announced that Mrs. Astor would be renting one of the Vanderbilt cottages on Point L'Acadie, Isle Cote, in Bar Harbor. As usual, young John Jacob Astor would accompany her, "the atmosphere agreeing well with his babyship," wrote the

Bar Harbor Record. Madeleine would once again be accompanied by her mother and sister. Also spending the summer in the area were notables such as Andrew Carnegie and George Lauder, Pittsburgh steel magnates. "Mrs. Astor apparently will take a very prominent part in society this summer," the *Bar Harbor Record* wrote.

That year Madeleine enjoyed frequent riding and motor trips, and visited both the Swimming Club and Kebo Valley Golf Club nearly every day. She was a guest at the first dinner of the season held at the Kebo Valley clubhouse. People could see that she was starting to make up for her quiet mourning period. "[S]he was the acknowledged leader of society, and both the Swimming Club and the Kebo [Valley] Golf Club were almost daily visited by her," wrote the *Bar Harbor Times.* "In fact, after an extremely quiet period after the *Titanic* disaster, it seemed that when convention and her own desires allowed, she intended to make up for the gloomy years that she had spent after the ocean tragedy," wrote the *Bar Harbor Times.*

Starting on July 11, Mrs. Astor and her sister became part of a group of summer residents called the War Relief Committee of Bar Harbor, who spent every day from ten a.m. to one p.m., except Sundays, making items to help the soldiers who were fighting in World War I. The town's high school building was turned over to the endeavor. Desks were removed from the school rooms and tables put in their place, where women and men worked side by side. The group made surgical dressings, bandages, and shirts for the wounded, together with garments of all kinds for refugees. Everything they made was delivered through the American Red Cross.

After an initial mix-up, year-round residents were assured they were also welcome to help. In the first two weeks, 5,500 surgical dressings and bandages were made, along with 434 finished garments. In the last two weeks of the five-week endeavor, 12,649 dressings and bandages were made, along with a total of 924 garments in that same period. "The noteworthy fact about these figures is that they indicate not a falling off of interest, such as might be expected in the gayest week of the season, but a great increase," wrote the *Bar Harbor Record.* The report also noted that other summer resorts were not doing the same thing for war-relief efforts.

On the evening that the committee began its work, Mrs. Astor gave a dinner for twenty guests. Three days later Mrs. Astor was a guest at the first of the weekly dances held at the Malvern Hotel, along with an exceptionally large gathering of high-society guests.

In July the *Bar Harbor Times* ran an untrue story about Mrs. Astor. Some newspapers had reported that Mrs. John Jacob Astor was at a New Haven hotel, passing through on a motor trip. According to the story, she had her pet poodle "Mizzie" with her. Because the hotel could not accommodate the dog, she sent her pet to another hotel—but only after ordering a steak, which was to be cut up in small pieces. "This kind of stuff helps to fill up the columns of the big Sunday editions, but as Mrs. Astor has been in Bar Harbor for the past month, the story falls pretty flat to those who know it to be false," wrote the *Bar Harbor Times.*

On July 15, Mrs. John Jacob Astor was a patroness for the Hampton meeting, held at the cottage of another summer colonist. It was attended by both summer and year-round residents alike. Miss Emily Slocum, the granddaughter of Henry Ward Beecher, spoke on the folk music of the African American race, giving a few explanatory sentences for each song presented. Captain Scott, a "Negro" graduate of Hampton, then made a short plea for the institution. Mr. Markine, an Apache Indian, also spoke.

Mrs. Astor attended many teas, luncheons, and dances, and hosted parties of her own that year. It was reported that trap shooting was becoming popular at the Country Club, enjoyed by

Mrs. Astor and the Pulitzers. In August she passed several days with Mrs. Joseph E. Widener in Newport before returning to Bar Harbor, where she continued her athletic pursuits.

Late in August Mrs. John Jacob Astor took a party—including her sister, H. O. Sturgis, and Mr. William Dick, a friend from her girlhood days in Brooklyn—to the Beech Hill cliff, which towers over Echo Lake. The group carried sandwiches, and she lit a huge bonfire to broil the thirty lamb chops they were also carrying. Mrs. Astor was standing near the edge of the precipice cooking her chop, which she was having trouble with. Upon the advice of the others, she put her chop closer in the fire, but it burned, while the others were all eating. She ended up throwing that chop into Echo Lake. She put another one on the fire, and within a few minutes she had satisfied herself that she could cook.

In September Mrs. John Jacob Astor helped to organize an event at a fellow summer colonist's cottage, where music and films were played to benefit the Polish Relief Fund.

"Her cottage was a center of gaiety all summer, and it was not till November, almost Thanksgiving Day, when she went back to New York—almost the last of the cottagers here to close their summer home," wrote the *Bar Harbor Times.* Mrs. Astor had finally arrived in society, and she was enjoying every minute of it.

"Her marriage to Col. Astor, whom she won solely by her beauty and charm, at once placed her in a position to dictate to the resort here and families who would have gladly snubbed her as plain Madeleine Force, were forced to recognize her unques-tioned social leadership as Mrs. John Jacob Astor and mother of the heir to the Astor millions. Since her marriage, her social posi-tion has been unquestioned here."

Mrs. Astor and her son, along with her sister, spent most of the winter of 1915–16 in Aiken, South Carolina, at a cottage Mrs. Astor owned. In May of 1916 it was announced that she and her son were expected in Bar Harbor at an early date, and would again be at the cottage on Vanderbilt Point. She arrived on the morning train of June 17, and her party was taken to Isle Cote, where she opened the cottage. Shortly after their arrival came a great rainstorm, keeping her indoors.

This was not going to be a typical summer for Mrs. Astor, however. Unbeknownst to the other summer colonists, she was due to remarry—and thus, forfeit her inheritance—the day after she arrived.

Her secret fiancé was Mr. William Dick, twenty-eight years old, the grandson of a sugar refiner and vice president of the Manufacturers Trust Company. Their relationship had begun as a childhood romance in Brooklyn, and had been revived again the previous winter in Aiken, South Carolina, where they were constantly in one another's company. At the time they had vigorously denied rumors of their engagement.

Madeleine Astor and William Dick had been engaged for two months prior to their June 1916 wedding. Their most intimate friends knew of the impending marriage, but great pains had been taken to keep it secret from the rest of the world.

Mr. Dick had called at Mrs. Astor's cottage several times the previous summer, one of many guests entertained there that season, including during the lamb chop incident. He was a guest at several occasions with Mrs. Astor in 1915, but no one had suspected a thing, just as no one was suspicious when her name had been coupled with those of half a dozen other men.

Mrs. Astor and Mr. Dick had intended to arrive in Bar Harbor on June 17, get a marriage license, and have a small wedding ceremony the following day. Her summer cottage was fully decorated, and arrangements had been made with local caterers and village businessmen, all under the promise of secrecy. Reservations had been made for a breakfast to be served for fifteen guests at a local hotel on the morning of the ceremony.

The day before the planned wedding, Mrs. Astor and Mr. Dick motored to the De Gregoire Hotel to make arrangements for a luncheon. The menu and decorations were in keeping with the simple tone of the nuptials. In order to guard her secrecy, Mrs. Astor initially told her caterer she was expecting friends on a yacht. After making the arrangements, she went motoring, for the first time in colors, wearing a rose-colored coat and a small black hat trimmed with white flowers.

Although the wedding plans had been meticulously made, a 1913 Maine statute revision—requiring a five-day wait before a marriage license could be granted in the case of nonresidents— made a mess of the plans. A New York lawyer had advised Mrs. Astor that the statute revision was a mere technicality that could be overlooked, so Madeleine and William headed to the Eden city hall to apply for their license.

There, Mrs. Astor's attention was called to the provision of the Maine law. "You may obtain the license next Thursday—not sooner," said the official who waited on them.

"But we must have a license for Monday," replied Mrs. Astor. "We're to be married Monday at Bar Harbor."

"Quite impossible," said the clerk. "The law is the law, and it can't be done."

Mrs. Astor pleaded with the clerk, telling him of the many plans that had been made: Guests were already on their way to her summer home, and the decorations were already in place, including flowers that would not last five days. She also expressed her need for complete secrecy. The clerk was not swayed.

Mrs. Astor returned to her summer cottage and immediately got on the phone and started sending telegraphs. She spent hours communicating with New York friends who were about to leave for the island. Her last call was to the lawyer who had given her the bad advice.

Because of the delay, it was initially believed that Mrs. Astor would return to New York and have the ceremony there, but this did not happen.

Nevertheless, her secret was out.

The date of the wedding was changed to Saturday. There was no formal wedding breakfast. A luncheon was hosted at the De Gregoire Hotel by Mr. Dick, given for members of his family. Tables were decorated with Killarney roses and a background of white lilacs, great masses of them, fragrant and creamy. Mr. Dick was accompanied at the breakfast by his father and mother, his two sisters and their husbands, a brother, and his uncle and aunt, along with others. At the same time, Mrs. Astor was holding a family gathering at Isle Cote, including her parents and sister, along with a few others. The train to Ellsworth was delayed an hour, delaying the wedding guests' arrival on the island and thereby shortening the luncheons.

Immediately after the meals were done, the parties took to their cars and headed to Bar Harbor's St. Saviour's Episcopal Church. The wedding guests numbered slightly over twenty. The cat out of the bag, a crowd of several hundred curious people were waiting outside the front of the church, including a battery of moving-picture men and their cameras, large and small.

The bridal party entered the church at two p.m., Mrs. Astor on her father's arm. There was no music, but there was the cooing of hundreds of doves who had made their home in the steeple for years, with the afternoon light filtering in through the stained-glass windows. Mrs. Astor wore a simple suit of blue serge, gray spats, black shoes, a simple little black hat trimmed with ribbon, and a magnificent set of silver gray fox furs. Her engagement ring was a large emerald surrounded by diamonds. The groom wore conventional afternoon dress.

Adolph Dick was the only attendant, acting as the best man, and Mrs. Astor was given away by her father, William H. Force. Young Astor was present at the ceremony.

The ceremony was brief, with the reading of the Episcopal service by Reverend Mr. Larned—featuring the word *obey*—as the main focus of the event. "[A]nd in a few minutes the widowed survivor of the *Titanic* was a bride once more, a radiant, thoroughly happy bride," wrote the *Bar Harbor Record.*

After the ceremony, one or two guests came conspicuously down the front walk and entered awaiting carriages. Onlookers rushed to the pathway, but no one else came out the front door. The only person they saw was a man named Edward Suminsby, guarding the entrance to the church. At the same time, several cars had been driven up Kennebec Street to the rear of the church, where the wedding party escaped the prying eyes of the public.

A look of disappointment came over the faces of the awaiting crowd when they realized they had been fooled. There was a mad rush for the back of the church, but it was all over. Newspaper-men took to their cars to chase the wedding party, but they were too late.

The crowd of Bar Harbor residents out front felt they had not been treated right. A ninety-six-year-old woman named "Grand-ma" Harris hobbled back to her home, declaring she had waited all her life to see a young woman who was willing to forfeit $5 million for love; unfortunately, she had missed her chance.

Immediately after the wedding, the bridal party drove to Ells-worth, where they boarded a train for New York. The Dicks were to spend a three-week honeymoon in Santa Barbara, California, in an attractive rose-covered bungalow, and would divide the rest of the summer between Bar Harbor and Mr. Dick's home on Long Island. Mrs. Force and Katherine remained at Isle Cote with young Astor, who was described as being on good terms with his new stepfather.

By her remarriage, Madeleine had forfeited all rights to her $5 million trust fund, which would return to the residuary estate, as well as use of the Fifth Avenue mansion and the rest of her inheritance.

Madeleine's time in Bar Harbor had essentially come to an end after her marriage to Mr. Dick. The Dicks went on to have two sons, William and John, but in 1933, they would obtain a Reno divorce.

Madeleine traveled abroad that year and met Italian middle-weight boxer Enzo Fiermonte. She was forty; he was twenty-six. They were married in a New York hospital, where Madeleine was a patient due to a broken shoulder she had suffered after a fall on a highly polished floor in her home in Bermuda. Mrs. Force was there, as were Madeleine's three sons, along with a few other family members and friends. A party in honor of the Fiermontes was held at the Newport Casino, but half of the resorters declined to attend.

Also in 1933, young Astor reached the age of twenty-one and came into possession of his inheritance. He was spending the summer with his aunt Katherine and her husband, Mr. Lorillard Spencer, at the time. He spent most of his birthday motoring to Newport from New Hampshire, and there was no special birthday observance.

The following year John Jacob Astor VI married Ellen Tuck French, a relative of the Pulitzer family, in Newport. There had been some doubt as to whether his mother would attend, but she arrived in Newport the night before, staying at a cottage named Chetwode. Her new husband was not with her. Mrs. Fiermonte sat in the front pew, attired in a gown of blue organdy and a large hat. She was escorted in and out of the church by her son, William Dick Jr.

In another pew sat Astor's former stepfather, William Dick Sr., along with their other son, John Henry Dick. Grandmother Force was also there.

Madeleine spent the winter of 1937–38 at a newly acquired home in South Carolina, at the Dixie Plantation, which had moss-hung oaks and faced a wide expanse of marsh and inland creeks. Madeleine had completely restored the house. Her happiness was to be short-lived, however, as she would divorce Fiermonte in 1938, saying only that "he had beaten her." To make matters worse, Dixie Plantation burned to the ground in 1939.

Later that year Madeleine went to Newport, renting a house on Bellevue Avenue, on which her son John Henry Dick also owned a home.

In January of 1940, Madeleine would lease Casa Invierno for the season, located on Jungle Road in Palm Beach, Florida. This followed several months of ill health that had prevented her from taking part in any social life.

On March 27, 1940, at 7:10 p.m., Madeleine died unexpectedly within thirty minutes of suffering a sudden heart attack. Her son, William Dick Jr., was at her bedside.

She was not quite forty-seven years old.

Madeleine's son John Henry Dick was born in 1919 and died in 1995. The choice of his first name was ironic. John loved nature, and his parents encouraged his outdoor pursuits. He was especially fascinated by birds, and married this interest with his skill as an artist, becoming a bird illustrator. John said his childhood was saddened by family conflicts, among other things; he and his brother Billy would often ask their mother about her *Titanic* adventure, but, he said, "She had little to tell."

Vincent Astor was a prominent summer resident of Northeast Harbor, the socially more quiet part of Mount Desert Island, residing at Cove's End. Vincent's third wife was Mrs. Mary Brooke Russell Marshall. Astor and Marshall were married in Bar Harbor in 1953 in a small ceremony, attended by a few friends and relatives, performed at the Pulitzer home.

In 1959 Vincent Astor died of a heart attack at the age of sixty-seven. He was buried in the same location in New York as his father. Vincent Astor left most of his money to the Astor Foundation, a philanthropic agency he had set up "to alleviate human misery." The Astor mansion is now the site of the Empire State Building.

John Jacob Astor VI died in June 1992 at his home in Miami Beach, at age seventy-nine. He worked briefly after graduating from school, but never again. He was married three times and divorced twice. He left a son, William, a daughter, Jacqueline, and three grandchildren.

Astor and his half-brother, Vincent, were not close. As a child, John Astor would spend a weekend or two with Vincent each year, which only served to upset Vincent. "He had the legal—not the moral—right to keep all the money," John Astor once said of his half-brother, Vincent.

Upon Vincent's death, John Astor hired a documents expert to study Vincent's twenty-seven-page will for erasures or insertions. None were found. He then charged that his half-brother was mentally incompetent at the time the will had been drawn up. With no chance of this charge being upheld, he then asked for a settlement of $2.5 million, but ultimately agreed to $250,000. John Astor said he did not want the money for himself, but for his children.

After her death, Vincent's widow left money to several Mount Desert Island institutions, including $50,000 for the Northeast Harbor Library, where she was a trustee.

XII

Hudson Trevor Allison was born in 1911 in Quebec. He was nearly a year old when he traveled on *Titanic* with his father, Hudson, a banker, and his mother, Bess, along with his two-year-old sister Lorraine, their nurse, Alice Cleaver, and other servants. Lorraine Allison had played in the Verandah Café with Winter Harbor resident Douglas Spedden, using it as a playroom.

After the *Titanic*'s impact with the iceberg, the Allisons had been awakened by a knock at their door from the adjoining stateroom, which was occupied by the children and their servants. Mr. Allison dismissed the concern of his son's nanny, Alice Cleaver, who later tried to go back again to rouse the rest of the family. They ignored her pleas. The nanny eventually returned to the deck with Trevor and escaped in a lifeboat.

Later, the rest of the party headed to the deck, but Mrs. Allison was separated from her husband, who had Lorraine. Mrs. Allison was put in a boat, but without her husband, and not knowing where Trevor was, she refused to leave the ship, and climbed out of the lifeboat.

Trevor was the only member of the Allison family to survive the sinking.

"When on Thursday night the nurse and her precious bundle entered the Hotel Manhattan, women and men in the lobby wept. "Yesterday morning when Baby [Trevor] was taken out, the unconcerned little survivor had no conception of the manner in which his orphaned plight was playing on the sentiments of many persons in the hotel," wrote the *New York Times*. "He was here only a few hours, but there wasn't a person here who went to bed Thursday night without a lot of thinking about that little chap," said the hotel's manager.

Hudson Trevor Allison died on Seaside Avenue in Old Orchard Beach, Maine, on August 7, 1929. He was just eighteen years old at the time. He had been visiting relatives there for five weeks. The cause of death was listed as acute ptomaine poisoning, contracted in Franklin, Massachusetts, where he had been visiting an aunt and uncle before coming to Maine.

In 2005 Mrs. Candee's family put up for auction the flask and the miniature cameo that had survived the sinking. The items were expected to go for between eight and twelve thousand pounds.

Candee continued to write throughout her life, penning such titles as *Angkor the Magnificent*. "But why go to Angkor—it is so far off the beaten track? asks petulantly the globe-girdler who keeps dates with his encircling steamer," wrote Candee. "That is why. You have said it. Because it *is* so far off the beaten track. I go there with a piqued interest, because it is the fruit so hard to pluck."

She lived at Coventry Hall in York Village, Maine, with her daughter and son-in-law, from 1945 until her death in 1949, at age ninety, after a brief illness. Candee was buried in the York Village Cemetery.

Eleanor Danforth was unable to sail again on *Carpathia* after it landed its *Titanic* survivors in New York because her companion was unable to accompany her. Instead, she sailed on April 25 on the RMS *Saxonia.*

The last listing for Eleanor Danforth was in the Gardiner, Maine, City Directories (1913–1925), at which time she lived with her father at 29 Pleasant Street in Gardiner. After 1915 she disappeared from the directory.

Myra Haxtun Harper died in 1923 at the age of sixty. In 1928, Mr. Harper, after an absence, would return to Harper and Brothers as a member of the board of directors, remaining there until his death. That year Harper purchased The Lodge, Seaview, on Mount Desert Island, which would be bought in 1975 by F. E. Dixon Jr., husband of Eleanor Widener.

By now Harper had remarried, to a woman named Anne Hopson. This Mrs. Harper was actively involved in improving the lives of area children, at one point hiring a local man to teach carpentry so that the children could build cabins on Turtle Island. She hired another man to tell stories and sing songs.

In his later years, Mr. Harper was afflicted with palsy. In his old age, he would often be seen riding in an open car around Grindstone Village, his hair waving in the breeze. He died in 1944 at the age of seventy-nine. Winter Harbor was listed as his summer home at the time of his death. He left a son, Henry, who was eighteen at the time of his death, and was training to become an officer in the navy.

Clara Hays's grandson, the product of the difficult pregnancy that had brought the Hays family back to the United States on *Titanic,* was born on April 23, 1912, and was named Thornton Davidson for his uncle who had been lost on *Titanic.*

The Grand Trunk Railway finished its plans to reach the Pacific on April 7, 1914, two years after *Titanic* sank, but the cost sent the company into bankruptcy. The railroad was taken over by the Canadian government.

In 1922, Mrs. Agnes Hale, a newcomer to Cushing Island, was invited along with other guests to the Hays house, to play tennis and have tea. When they arrived, Clara Hays was sitting on the big, enclosed porch of the home she and her late husband had built for their retirement, pouring tea into thin Indian Tree china cups. Mrs. Hays welcomed her guests warmly.

Mrs. Hale described Mrs. Hays as a charming, handsome woman whose pleasure it was to run a large, well-staffed house for her children and grandchildren, and also to maintain warm friendships with all the islanders, especially the younger ones.

That afternoon Mrs. Hays urged all of her guests to eat freely of the sandwiches, cakes, and hot biscuits her staff had prepared. She served a cake that had been baked into the shape of a fallen tree trunk, heavily iced with chocolate and trimmed with maraschino cherries, a small hatchet-like knife lying beside it. Mrs. Hays told Mrs. Hale that her cook, although very good, had to be watched and appraised every day in order to keep her culinary performances up to standard. In Mrs. Hays's opinion, Canadian cooks could not cook like Southerners.

Mr. Hays's sister, Miss Mary Hays—known as Aunt Mame— had lived in the Hays household ever since the four Hays girls had begun to grow up and go around as young ladies. This was partly because chaperoning and managing four girls was too much for Mrs. Hays alone, especially since she traveled so often with her husband. After Charles Hays's death, Aunt Mame continued to keep company with Clara.

The two women spent their summers at the island sitting on the front porch in the morning, the living room at teatime. They truly enjoyed young people, and liked to be in the thick of things. They had an innate love of mischief, a gleam in their eyes—a constant flame of barely suppressed excitement. They never moralized or condemned, so they always got full reports of the youngsters' activities.

With her household full of married daughters and grandchildren, Mrs. Hays always needed to employ at least seven servants, including a chauffeur, gardener, and yard boy. Mrs. Hays's secretary ruled over the staff. In 1927 Mrs. Hays gave a party to celebrate the island's emancipation from the use of kerosene with the arrival of electricity. Clara did not allow the playing of tennis on her Cushing Island courts until well into the 1930s.

Mrs. Hays died in 1955 at the age of ninety-five. Her four daughters survived her. Daughter Orian Davidson, who would remarry after losing her husband on *Titanic*, died in 1979, at the age of ninety-six.

A plaque hangs in the first Unitarian Church in Buffalo, a building designed by architect Edward A. Kent: IN MEMORY OF EDWARD AUSTIN KENT, BANGOR, MAINE, FEB. 19, 1854—SS *TITANIC*, APRIL 15, 1912.

A large stone in the Mattawamkeag Cemetery reads CHARLES L. KIRKLAND, BURIED AT SEA, 1843–1912. Also listed are the names of his wife, Rachel, and children Grace, George, and Pearl, the latter three having died in 1888.

The Kirklands had sent a description of their father to the Halifax Police Department to aid in his possible identification. He was never identified. Son Algie L. Kirkland would file suit against the owners of *Titanic* on behalf of the family. He listed his father as a resident of Old Town, Maine, and said he died without a will. According to the document, he left no widow. They listed damages at $4,000.

Dr. Alice Leader retired from medicine in the 1920s, and spent her last four winters in Florida with her sister, where she died in April of 1944, following a four-day illness.

William Sloper told his father he felt like he ought to sue the Hearst paper for slander for the story identifying him as having escaped *Titanic* dressed as a woman. The elder Mr. Sloper said it was not worthwhile. Sloper would continue to receive anonymous letters with newspaper clippings enclosed for years to come. He recalled: "In the letters themselves the senders called me all kinds of names for not staying on the sinking ship and going down with it."

Two weeks after returning home, several of Sloper's friends organized a dinner party to celebrate his escape from *Titanic*. The host of the party was especially proud of the table's centerpiece— a tank holding several cakes of ice, in the center of which floated a small, three-masted toy clipper ship.

Everywhere Sloper went for at least the next two years, someone would ask him about *Titanic*. "I was to stand up to a barrage of the same questions I had answered many times before, and to hear myself giving the same answers over and over again."

Sloper would spend the winter following the *Titanic* disaster on his usual vacation, traveling in Egypt. He often ran into J. P. Morgan there that winter, Morgan's last on Earth. For two weeks Sloper would often sit near Morgan at the Shepheard Hotel in Cairo. "I could easily see into the remarkable eyes of this amazing man. Those eyes reminded me of two quick-firing cannon, one on each side of an aeroplane nose, as they looked out at everyone and everything from behind the Morgan bulbous proboscis."

One night in May 1926, Sloper boarded a Pullman sleeping car bound for a trout-fishing expedition in Greenville, Maine. That night the voice of his subconscious took hold of him, insisting that Sloper listen—that he should leave the stock market business "while the going was good." The stock market would crash a few years later.

Sloper married three years after the sinking. In 1926, Mr. Sloper and his wife were returning from Europe on the SS *Olympic,* where, on Sunday, April 14, the ship arrived at the site of *Titanic*'s sinking. Those on board the *Olympic* held a brief ceremony in honor of those who were lost.

William T. Sloper died suddenly at age seventy-one on May 1, 1955, at his home in Hartford, Connecticut, after a cerebral hemorrhage. He was well-known in financial circles, and had been active in the investment brokerage business in New Britain and Hartford for many years. He was a member of the First Baptist Church and the Sons of the American Revolution. He served a term on the Common Council many years before his death, and was a country club organizer. He left a wife, Mrs. Helen Tallmadge, a half-brother, Erwin Sloper, of Maine, and several nieces and nephews.

William's half-brother Erwin, who would become an innkeeper in Greenville, would marry Mrs. Anne Louise Baxter from New York. The "Sloper House" still stands on Blair Hill in Greenville, directly across the Lily Bay Road, now known as Blair Hill Inn. Formally called the Lakeview House Bed and Breakfast, the inn features the Sloper Room.

Two days after the *Titanic* sank, on April 17, 1912, J. P. Morgan celebrated his seventy-fifth birthday. The summer of the sinking, Morgan came to Mount Desert Island in July of 1912, cruising along the coast in *Corsair,* going to "Bishop Doane's Church," having lunch at the Doanes' house, and spending time with his family. While there, J. P. Morgan attended the horse show.

Morgan would die a year after *Titanic* sank, and his funeral would be held exactly a year after *Titanic*'s sinking.

During the summer after the sinking, the Spedden family took their usual cottage, the Bonsall Taylor cottage in Winter Harbor, coming from Morristown, New Jersey.

The Speddens had led a seemingly charmed life both before and immediately after the *Titanic* disaster, escaping the sinking unscathed. At about six p.m. on August 6, 1915, however, during the last summer that Madeleine Astor would spend in Bar Harbor, the Spedden family's luck would change.

Douglas Spedden, now age nine, had been playing in front of their summer cottage with a tennis ball. The ball got away from him, and, as children do, Douglas followed quickly, inattentively, after it. He emerged from the thick shrubbery that grew close to one side of the street, colliding with an automobile. The driver of the car, Foster Harrington, a Winter Harbor native who was twenty-six at the time of the accident, was unable to avoid Douglas because of the closeness of the entrance and the small distance between the car and the child.

Harrington picked up the unconscious boy and carried him to his home. Douglas regained consciousness the next day, but by that night, his condition had worsened, and the next morning Dr. William Sawyer, Winter Harbor physician, pronounced the boy dead. "The accident has cast a gloom over the entire village of Winter Harbor and Grindstone, where the little fellow was universally liked," wrote the *Bar Harbor Times*. "It is the first automobile fatality in that vicinity."

F. E. Sherman, the Bar Harbor undertaker who years earlier had tended to the elder Mrs. Widener, took care of the arrangements, which included a burial three days later in New York. Harrington was held blameless and was not charged with any crime.

The Speddens kept coming back to spend their summers in Maine, but they changed their summer home from Winter Harbor to Northeast Harbor, presumably to avoid reminders of the horrible accident. They often stayed at Northeast Harbor's Kimball House.

The *Titanic* disaster did nothing to dull Mr. Spedden's interest in the water. Described as a keen yachtsman, Spedden kept his own boat in the harbor. In 1923 he served as an official for the yacht races sponsored by the Bar Harbor Yacht Racing Committee, held in Frenchman Bay.

Sadly, water turned out to be Mr. Spedden's enemy in the end. He died in 1947, experiencing a heart attack while swimming in a pool in Palm Beach, Florida, where he was spending the winter.

In 1950, the *Bar Harbor Times* ran an obituary for Mrs. Spedden, who died on February 10 at her home in Tuxedo Park, New York, listing her as a *Titanic* survivor. The obituary also mentions that she and her husband spent their summers in Northeast Harbor, where Mr. Spedden was a great sailboat enthusiast.

Jack Thayer gave two interviews after leaving *Carpathia*—the first, on the same night as his arrival. According to the article, "Mother and I were about to go to bed when we were thrown headlong to the floor of our stateroom. Before we knew what had happened, terrible screams seemed to come from every direction."

His father quickly came to their aid, getting them quickly up on deck. "Men and women were running in all directions, and everyone was excited. Women fainted, and the cry was soon sent up that the *Titanic* had struck an iceberg." His mother was unnerved by the accident. Deckhands shouted that there was no danger, which calmed many. An officer grabbed his mother and dragged her to a lifeboat. She reached out and clutched her son's arm, leading him over to the officer who was loading the lifeboats.

"By this time men and women were bidding good-bye to one another," Thayer recalled. "I heard the shouts of the crew that all men must stand back, and as Mother was placed in a lifeboat, I freed myself from her grasp and told her not to worry. 'All men must remain,' I called to her, 'and I will stay with Father.'"

Mrs. Thayer continued to beg him to come with her, even as the lifeboat was being lowered. Thayer said he waved good-bye and returned to his father's side.

"For the next hour or so nothing could be heard on deck but screams, sobs, and curses. The crew and passengers ran in all directions. Father and I remained together, and when we all knew that the boat was going to sink, he put a life preserver around my neck and told me to jump for my life.

"I will follow," the elder Thayer said.

Young Thayer jumped. He floated among wreckage until he was almost frozen to death. Eventually, he grabbed hold of a big stick of wood. Thayer continued to think of his father, and those thoughts numbed his physical pain. He eventually lost consciousness, floating in the water until a small boat came and picked him up.

The next day, however, surrounded by his family and officers of the Pennsylvania Railroad, Jack Thayer's story was somewhat different for a *New York Times* reporter. The new version was more like the 1940 account Thayer wrote for his immediate family, which has subsequently been published. It was dedicated to the memory of his father.

"The whole event passes before me now, in 1940, as vividly and with the same clarity as twenty-eight years ago, in 1912. And due to the great size of modern ships, no two individuals, no matter how close they may [have been] together on shipboard, have the same description of [the] experience to relate, should they [have been] so fortunate as to [have survived] the ordeal," wrote Thayer.

Jack Thayer wrote of how his life had been planned out for him by his father, beginning with college, followed by an apprenticeship in a banking house overseas. "It could be planned. It was planned. It was a certainty.

"Today the individual has to be contented with rapidity of motion, nervous emotion, and economic insecurity. To my mind the world of today awoke April 15, 1912."

Jack Thayer began paying calls to Lois Cassatt in Bar Harbor after the *Titanic* sank, at least as early as 1915. Lois Cassatt was a summer visitor and granddaughter of the builder of the Pennsylvania Railroad, Mr. A. J. Cassatt, of Haverford, Pennsylvania. Jack and Lois were married in 1923. Their summer cottage was Cover Farm in Hulls Cove. Their phone number was 533. They were members of the Kebo Valley Golf Club, among other island institutions.

Thayer served as the financial vice president of the University of Pennsylvania. His son, Edward C. Thayer, was killed at age twenty while fighting in the Southwest Pacific during World War II. Thayer died shortly after his son was killed in the war, apparently of a self-inflicted gunshot wound. His family still has an active presence on the island today.

Peter Arrell Brown Widener, who died in 1915, would spend the last three years of his life grief-stricken over the loss of his son and grandson, although he did find some comfort while sailing on his yacht.

Widener's grandson Harry had collected rare books, and his collection included a rare Shakespeare folio and a Gutenberg Bible. Harry had been purchasing books overseas before sailing on *Titanic*. P. A. B. Widener would spend time completing that collection, and Harry's mother, Eleanor, would build a library at Harvard, from which Harry graduated, for the books. At the 1913 commencement ceremony, the cornerstone for the library was laid, with this inscription: "Harry Elkins Widener A. B. 1907. Loved the books which he had collected and the college to which he bequeathed them. He laboured not for himself only but for all those who seek learning. This memorial has been placed here by his classmates."

Eleanor would later remarry. She died in 1937 of a heart attack in a Paris department store, at the age of seventy-five.

The Wideners' daughter, the younger Eleanor—for whom Mrs. Widener had been purchasing a trousseau in Europe before boarding *Titanic*—would marry F. Eugene Dixon, known as Genie to his friends. The Dixons spent some summers in Newport with her mother, but once Eleanor Jr. came to Grindstone in Winter Harbor, she spent almost every summer there until her death in 1966. The Dixons had two children, and were later divorced.

The younger Eleanor died at age seventy-four in Pennsylvania. Among other charitable giving in the state, she would contribute to the Maine Coast Memorial Hospital and the Eleanor Widener Dixon Memorial Clinic in Gouldsboro.

Eva Shorey, the Portland reporter who had covered *Carpathia*'s arrival, died in 1964 at the age of ninety-two. She was the daughter of Major Henry A. and Ida Currier Shorey, and was born in Portland on July 6, 1871. She was a graduate of Bridgton High School and Gray's Business College in Portland.

Shorey served as a special agent of the Maine Bureau of Industrial and Labor Statistics, and in 1907 prepared a report on working women in Portland. The report concluded: "The woman wage-earner of Portland is a person, and not merely a screw in a machine, as she would be in a larger city." Among Shorey's stories was a three-part report on working conditions in Lewiston cotton mills, for the *Bridgton News* in 1908.

Shorey had served as a secretary to notable political figures and had traveled abroad before returning to Maine in 1914 to become the town correspondent for the *Portland Evening Ex-*

press. She also worked as a contributor to several other newspapers, including the *Bridgton News,* owned by her father, her brother, the late Henry A. Shorey Jr., and now, her nephew, Henry A. Shorey. She wrote a weekly column, "Looking South from My Window," which appeared for many years in the *Norway Advertiser-Democrat.* She served as the children's editor of the *Portland Evening Express.* In 1897 she was secretary to the speaker and secretary of the House of Representatives. From 1897 to 1904 she was secretary to the governor of Maine. She then worked for US Representative Edwin C. Burleigh until 1907, when she went to the State Labor Bureau.

Shorey was a lifelong Republican, active in the women's suffrage movement, and voted in every election for many years after women won the right to vote. She was a trustee of the Farragut Memorial Association, GAR. She never married or had children, and at the time of her death was survived by three nephews and two nieces.

In the news story covering her death, the first paragraph reads: "Miss Eva Lovering Shorey, who covered the sinking of the *Titanic . . .*"

On May 2, Richard White's body arrived in Massachusetts from Halifax on the one o'clock train. There was a brief service at the cemetery, followed by his burial in the White family lot. Mrs. White and Percival Jr. had come from Brunswick for the service, along with other family members. Nelson D. White & Sons closed for the day, and workers served as pallbearers for Richard's casket. On May 25 a memorial service was held in Massachusetts for Percival Sr., whose body was never recovered.

Responses quickly came in to the inquiry sent to survivors under the name of the cotton business, asking for any news about Percival and Richard's last minutes on the sinking ship.

They received a reply from Bruce Ismay, dated May 29:

I am in receipt of your letter of the 14th inst. from which I deeply regret to learn that you lost your brother Percival W. White and his son on the *Titanic,* and beg to tender you my very sincere sympathy in your bereavement.

I will certainly institute inquiries among the crew, stewards, and stewardesses and ascertain if any of them can give you any information in regard to your brother, and will advise you with what result. Believe me.

Yours truly,
Bruce Ismay

On May 7 Mrs. Elizabeth Lines wrote to Mrs. White. She knew one of Percival's brothers, saying their children had played together. Mrs. Lines said that because the families knew each other, she felt Percival and Richard were not strangers when they met on *Titanic.* "Indeed, ever since reaching New York I have felt I must write and tell Mrs. White how very kind and cordial her husband and son both were to my girlie and myself during those few days at sea," wrote Mrs. Lines.

Mrs. Lines wanted to tell the Whites of the many acts of kindness performed for her by the Whites, but settled on one. She said during the voyage, her daughter did not like being on the water, though it was calm, and spent Saturday in her stateroom. Percival wanted to do something for her, and at last proposed that Richard should play his mandolin for her. Mrs. Lines thought that was too much to ask a young man to do, but Richard did it, playing and singing for her little daughter for an hour. "I shall never forget it, and have wanted to tell his mother," Mrs. Lines wrote.

On the night of the sinking, with their staterooms right next to one another, Mrs. Lines heard Percival leave his stateroom a few minutes after the crash. Later he would go to her door and ask if she or her daughter were uneasy. She said she feared there was great danger to the vessel, but that her steward had reassured her and told her to return to bed. Mr. White had said there was ice up on deck, but that there was nothing to worry about. She would hear Mr. White leave his stateroom again, and about fifteen minutes later, she heard him calling, "Run for the lifeboats, Richard!"

When Mrs. Lines and her daughter reached the boat deck, they found Percival and Richard and two other friends already there. The Whites were fully dressed and had on overcoats and life preservers. They both were kind and reassuring and tried to talk calmly, but the noise of the escaping steam was almost deafening. Percival seemed very nervous, and moved off down the deck. The last thing Mrs. Lines heard him say was "Keep close to me, Richard."

Mrs. Lines said there was no message sent back home because few people thought the ship would actually sink, and they had been told steamers would be at their aid in a short period of time.

On *Carpathia* she had looked for the Whites and asked about them, and a few passengers said they had seen father and son together on deck. "I wish I could tell you more, but the Terror of the wreck seemed to numb us all," she wrote. She added that she and her daughter felt like they had lost dear friends with the loss of the Whites. "[W]e have truly mourned with you," she said in closing.

Algernon H. Barkworth wrote that he, along with another man, had helped to tie on Percival's life belt. Barkworth was under the impression that Percival was sleeping at the time of the crash, and had dressed hurriedly before coming on deck.

"He appeared to me to be very nervous and excited, and the sweat was pouring off his face like rain," Barkworth wrote. He said that when he saw him, his hair was in disorder, and he never wore a hat.

Passenger Jean Hippach wrote and said that she had met the Whites through Mrs. Lines on the second day of the voyage. Mrs. Hippach teasingly called Richard "Richward." She said they had many pleasant visits, and played whist together after lunch. She said Richard played the mandolin beautifully, and just as beautifully sang all his college songs for them. "We enjoyed them so much," Hippach wrote.

Hippach said that she and her mother were going up the stairs to the lifeboats after the crash and met both Whites on the way. She told Richard she was dreadfully frightened, while she found Percival Sr. and Richard not the least bit concerned. "Oh, there is no need for that," replied Richard with a comforting smile.

The Whites escorted Mrs. Hippach and her mother to the boat deck, where they waited for the same lifeboat as the Astors. Along with the millionaires' group, the Hippachs were ordered down to A Deck for final loading. The party, including Percival Sr. and Richard, walked together to A Deck, where all of the ladies were ordered to get into Lifeboat 4. Mrs. Hippach said she had hoped all four could get in one lifeboat, but the one they were offered was too crowded. She said they left the ship only twenty minutes before it went down.

"We will have some exciting things to talk about now," Richard said to her.

Mrs. Hippach and the Whites were told the *Olympic* had been sighted, and would pick them up in less than an hour. Percival had a bottle of wine with him, and gave Mrs. Hippach and her mother each a sip.

"It made Mother feel stronger, and I am very sure it is what kept Mother up during the dreadfully long night," wrote Mrs. Hippach.

On May 12 passenger George A. Brayton wrote the family to say that he was acquainted with the Whites because they ate at adjoining tables at mealtime, and he also saw them often on deck. He saw them after *Titanic* struck the iceberg, both fully dressed and with life belts on. Percival was doing all that could be done to help the women and children into the lifeboats, and seemed very cool. Brayton said a passenger on *Carpathia* had seen them in the water, and saw Percival go down.

Almost immediately after *Carpathia*'s arrival, hearings about the sinking of the *Titanic* began in the US Senate. The testimony of Frank Oliver Evans, a *Titanic* seaman, piqued the White family's interest. Evans testified that he had pulled a large man, who later died, into Lifeboat 14, from the overturned lifeboat that had also rescued young Jack Thayer. On May 17 Nelson D. White & Sons sent a picture of Percival to the White Star Line in England and asked them to show the picture to Evans to see if the man possibly was Percival.

On June 10, the White Star Line responded. They said they had found Evans, and that he at once had recognized the photograph of Mr. Percival W. White as that of the heavy gentleman who was taken into the lifeboat about two hours after *Titanic* sank.

"Mr. White was [barely] breathing when he was taken into the boat, and although Evans apparently did everything he could to revive him, he died within a few minutes after being got into the boat." The letter said that after the boat's survivors were picked up by *Carpathia,* Mr. White's body was buried at sea at about five o'clock in the afternoon of the same day, a burial service being held over his body.

After further communication, presumably concerning possessions found on the body, the White Star Line wrote the White family again on September 28. Of Evans, they said, "He is still strongly of the opinion that the body he picked up was that of the gentleman whose photograph you sent us, viz: Mr. Percival W. White. He knows nothing of what was found on the body, as it was taken on board the *Carpathia* and buried from that steamer."

The White Star Line official said that while they believed Evans, the captain of the *Carpathia*, reported that the body had not been buried from that steamer. The White Star Line suggested that someone might go to New York to speak with Evans when he sailed there in October.

"We may say that Evans has been at our disposal whenever he has been ashore on this matter, and has lost some little time in connection with same, which fact you will perhaps bear in mind if you should send someone to interview him in New York."

On June 5, Victor Sunderland, who had also been on the overturned lifeboat, wrote to the White family. He said that a man had climbed on their boat about ten minutes after the *Titanic* sank, with a life preserver on. Sunderland said that he thought the man was Percival W. White, and that he had died on the upturned boat about an hour before the lifeboats picked him up.

"I believe he must have left the *Titanic* before she sank, or else he would have drifted with the others in another direction," wrote Sunderland. He said that the only time he'd heard the man speak was when someone asked if all the people on the boat were crew, and the unidentified man answered that he was a passenger.

"I believe he joined in the prayers; there were for a time about thirty-five [on the boat], all men; when we were picked up, we numbered twelve. You may read reports [that say] thirty [were] saved from that boat, but they are not true."

Sunderland said that the man subsequently died, and his body was pushed off that boat after daylight.

On June 22, Colonel Archibald Gracie, part of Mrs. Candee's on-board party, who was also on the upturned boat, wrote to the White family. Gracie said he doubted the story about a body being pushed off the upturned boat. He said that when they were rescued by another lifeboat, the body was also loaded onto that rescue boat. Gracie had tried to revive the man, but said that rigor mortis had already set in. "The boat was so crowded that I lay on this man's body during the hour or more that it took to row the lifeboat to the *Carpathia*'s side," wrote Gracie.

Gracie said the man was dressed like a member of the crew, and that beyond doubt he wore gray woolen socks. Gracie said he repeatedly asked Lightoller about the identity of the body, and that Lightoller was equally sure he was a crew member. Gracie said the body was taken aboard *Carpathia,* where a funeral service was read over it, and several others.

"I feel akin to all you people who have suffered loss," wrote Gracie in the letter's conclusion.

On October 15, Gracie sent a letter directly to Edith White, in response to several letters she had written back to him. "I am convinced that your husband's body was not aboard the *Carpathia,*" wrote Gracie. "[The body referred to] had black hair and in no way resembled Mr. White. Your husband, therefore, it seems to me, was not one of those who suffered agony for hours and finally collapsed just before being saved," wrote Gracie. "His life was probably extinguished in an instant and without pain."

The Whites sued the White Star Line, and were able to provide, in the lawsuit, a list of possessions Percival had carried on the ship, valued at $1,000, including a watch chain, ring, gloves, two men's suits, a golf jacket, Liberty coat, pin, bracelet watch, liberty inkstand, liberty books, two liberty scarves, three neck chains, a jeweled chain, and cash and other articles.

After the sinking, Bowdoin College president Hyde spent much time with Mrs. White, and also playing with Matilda, Percival Jr.'s daughter, at The Pines, the Whites' home in Brunswick. Hyde had barely been acquainted with her at the time of the sinking.

"For six weeks after the blow fell he came to see her every day. He sometimes talked gently to her, that she might find some tolerable meaning in the event that had befallen. Sometimes he refrained from all reference to it, reading to her instead. But he never preached," wrote Charles Theodore Burnett in his book, *Hyde of Bowdoin.*

In 1931, Matilda was married at The Pines. A photograph that ran in the paper shows her in her wedding gown, standing at The Pines in front of a photograph hung on the wall of Percival, and an oil painting of Richard.

Mrs. White loaned Bowdoin College objects collected by Mr. White and members of his family during their travels, including marbles, bronzes, porcelain pieces, and oil and watercolor paintings. These were a memorial to her husband and son, and were placed in the school's Walker Art Building in a new lecture room to be used for a new course in art history. One was a painting of Richard at age six.

In 1942 there was a fire at The Pines, by this time deserted. The house had been under observation by the police because of two break-ins. The fire destroyed the White library. Family portraits, hanging in the stairwell nearby, were also destroyed by the intense heat. Statues and antiques were badly damaged. Upon the house's demolition after the fire, a neighbor, Mr. Murray Litchfield, found a locket with the initials PWW nestled in the grass on the front lawn. He donated the item to the Pejepscot Historical Society of Brunswick in the late 1990s.

Matilda would go on to attend Bowdoin, and in the 1970s served as the school's first woman full professor.

Just a few days after Richard's body had been identified on the *Mackay-Bennett,* at Bowdoin's Sunday church services, Richard's graduating class marched into the college chapel in their caps and gowns to a funeral march, and went to their accustomed places. The service included a responsive reading and a scripture lesson, including the comforting twenty-sixth chapter of St. John. A double quartet sang a song to the departed, and following the prayer, the class marched out, again to a funeral march. Mrs. White and Percival Jr. were present.

College president Hyde read a eulogy: "Richard Frasar White has left Bowdoin College a precious legacy," said Hyde. "If we can each appropriate our share, we shall be better men to the end of our days; and through us he may still do for the world something of what in his own person he was so splendidly prepared to do."

Hyde described White as the comrade of his father and the confidant of his mother, sharing with them their burdens and his problems, "so that their life and his were one." Hyde continued: "The intimacy of parents and son in this case is visibly attested [to] by the beautiful home built expressly that through the college years they might not lose this close companionship," said Hyde.

Hyde recounted how he had played golf with Richard, and during the many games, only once had Hyde won, beating also his own best score. "[Richard] knew the score was altogether out of my ordinary range. So he sent me a copy of the score, saying he thought I might like to keep it. I am glad now to have that thoughtful autograph as one more example of the 'little nameless unremembered acts of kindness and of love' of which his life was full."

Hyde described Richard's interests as apart from the ordinary, artificial interests most college students were supposed to have, noting that Richard had cared about literature, travel, and wood-working.

"We who have known him through almost an entire college course, can best express our gratitude and affection by adding to our own lives some portion of the frankness and fidelity, the earnestness and kindliness, the modesty and efficiency which in him we have admired and loved," said Hyde.

The graduation of Bowdoin's class of 1912 went on as scheduled, without Richard.

The true lesson of Richard White had not been lost on Frank Arthur Smith, who, a month after he had claimed Richard's body and witnessed the horror of Halifax, gave the closing address at commencement. Before the sinking, Richard had been criticized by his classmates as bookish, introverted, and pretentious. But Smith praised Richard in his speech:

> There remains one more great factor which has helped us in building well—that is the friendship of classmates. We all have been severed from the life of a dear, honored member of our class; and while we have much to be thankful for this day, our hearts go out in sympathy to the noble mother who yearns for the baby she so tenderly reared. While we are saddened by this vacant place within our ranks, yet our hearts swell with pride, and we think with greatest admiration of the nobility with which he met his death. "Greater love hath no man than this—that he lay down his life for his friends." The last minutes of Dick White's life were spent in assisting, assuring, and strengthening the hearts of the weak and helpless that they might live.

While men like Ismay jumped into lifeboats, and some were said to have dressed like women in order to save themselves; while some men jumped into lowering lifeboats, and others had to be stopped at gunpoint; Richard White stood back and followed the order of the sea, to be a gentleman, while his father helped to load lifeboats.

The rest of Bowdoin's Class of 1912 philosophized that their duty as Bowdoin men was the duty to fight for greater equality of opportunity, and to give every man his chance. In the moment of truth, the once-ostracized Richard White had lived up to this mission, at the cost of his own life.

Smith reminded his classmates of this fact at the graduation ceremony, which Richard, who had worked so hard to belong, could not be a part of.

> Men of the Class of 1912, we have the highest example life can furnish to measure up to, and the noble death of one of our number must bear fruit in our lives. So wherever we go, to whatever work we are called, whether great or small, may we,

too, catch Dick White's spirit with that forgetfulness of self, and trusting in life's great Pilot, may we answer with the best that is in us.

SOURCE LIST

Abbott Historical Society, Abbott, Maine.

Androscoggin Historical Society, Auburn, Maine.

Angkor the Magnificent, the Wonder City of Ancient Cambodia, by Helen Churchill Candee, Frederick A. Stokes Company, New York, 1924.

The Astor Family, John D. Gates, Doubleday and Company, Inc., Garden City, New York, 1981.

The Astors, by Harvey O'Connor, Alfred A. Knopf, New York, 1941.

The Astors, A Family Chronicle of Pomp and Power, by Lucy Havaler, Dodd, Mead & Company, New York.

Bangor Daily Commercial (newspaper).

Bangor Daily News (newspaper).

Bar Harbor Historical Society.

The Bar Harbor Record (newspaper).

The Bar Harbor Times (newspaper).

Bath Daily Times (newspaper).

Biddeford Weekly Journal (newspaper).

Biographical Directory of the United States Congress.

Boston Evening Transcript (newspaper).

Bowdoin Bugle (Bowdoin Class of 1912 yearbook).

Bowdoin College Orient (literary magazine).

Bradford Heritage: Museum and Historical Society, Bradford, Maine.

Brunswick Record (newspaper).

Buffalo and Erie County Historical Society, New York.

Buffalo Express (newspaper).

Chester Baptist Church, Chester, Maine.

City of Bangor, Department of Vital Statistics.

Congregational Church of East Sumner, East Sumner, Maine.

Cushing's Island, Two Memoirs, Robert and Agnes Hale, Copyright 1971.

Daily Eastern Argus (newspaper).

Daily Kennebec Journal (newspaper).

Danforth Baptist Church, Danforth, Maine.

Down to the Sea in Ships, by Helen Churchill Candee.

The Eastport Sentinel (newspaper).

The Ellsworth American (newspaper).

End of the Line, Alexander J. Cassatt and the Pennsylvania Railroad, by Patricia T. Davis, Neale Watson Academic Publications, Inc., New York, 1978.

Excerpts from "The Daily Journal of 'Daisy' Spedden; A Titanic Survivor," *The Titanic Commutator,* The Journal of the Titanic Historical Society, Inc., Volume 16, Number 3, November 1992, Indian Orchard, Massachusetts.

Gardiner City Directories.

The Gazette, Montreal (newspaper).

Good Old Summer Days, by Richmond Barrett, Houghton Mifflin Company, Boston 1952.

The Grand Trunk in New England, by Jeff Holt, 1986, Raifare Enterprises Limited, West Hill, Ontario, Canada.

The Halifax Herald (newspaper).

Harper's Weekly, May 4, 1912, Harper & Brothers, New York.

The Harvard Library and the Harry Elkins Widener Memorial Library Building, Harvard University Press, Cambridge, Massachusetts, 1921.

An Historical Sketch, Guide Book, and Prospectus of Cushing's Island, Casco Bay, Coast of Maine, by William M. Sargent, American Photo-Engraving Company, New York 1886.

Home From the Sea, by Sir Arthur H. Rostron, The MacMillan Company, New York, 1931.

How Women May Earn a Living, by Helen Churchill Candee, Cornell Library Historical Monographs.

Hyde of Bowdoin, by Charles T. Burnett, Houghton Mifflin Company, Boston and New York, 1931.

The Independent Reporter (newspaper; part of *The Somerset Independent* and *The Somerset Reporter*).

In Their Own Words, Titanic, by Charles Pellegrino, ebook, charlespellegrino.com/in_their_own_words.htm.

The Island City, A History of Eastport, Moose Island, Maine, by John "Terry" Holt.

J. Pierpont Morgan; An Intimate Portrait, by Herbert Livingston Satterlee, The MacMillan Company, New York, 1939.

Kennebec Historical Society.

Lewiston Daily Sun (newspaper).

Lewiston Evening Journal (newspaper).

The Life and Times of Andrew Jackson Sloper 1849-1933, W. T. Sloper, 1949.

The Life and Times of Nelson Dingley, Jr., by Edward Nelson Dingley, Ihling Bros & Everard, Kalamazoo, Michigan, 1902.

Lost Bar Harbor, G. W. Helfrich and Gladys O'Neil, Down East Books, Camden, Maine.

Maine State Archives.

A Man and the Paper Industry: Hugh J. Chisholm 1847-1912, The Newcomen Society in North America, 1952.

Moosehead Historical Museum, Greenville, Maine.

My World on an Island, by Sylvia M. Kuson, Down East Books, Camden, Maine 1982.

New York Times (newspaper).

New York Tribune (newspaper).

The Night Lives On, by Walter Lord, Avon Books, Inc., New York 1986.

A Night to Remember, by Walter Lord, Bantam Books, 1955.

1910 Maine Census.

The Old Town Enterprise (newspaper).

Old York Historical Society.

Other Edens: The Sketchbook of an Artist Naturalist, by John Henry Dick, Devin-Adair Company, Old Greenwich, Connecticut, 1979.

Palm Beach Times (newspaper).

Parkman Baptist Church, Parkman, Maine.

Parkman Historical Society, Parkman, Maine.

Philadelphia Inquirer (newspaper).

The Pilgrim Way, Marion Edna Reed Kimball, House of Falmouth, Portland, Maine, 1962.

Polar, The Titanic Bear, by Daisy Corning Stone Spedden, Madison Press, Produced for Little, Brown and Company, 1992, 1994.

Portland Evening Express (newspaper).

Portland Evening Express and Advertiser (newspaper).

Portland Press Herald (newspaper).

The Pejepscot Historical Society, Brunswick, Maine.

Public Archives of Nova Scotia.

The Quill, literary magazine of Bowdoin College, Brunswick, Maine.

The Republican Journal (newspaper).

Rumford Falls Times (newspaper).

Saint John Globe (newspaper).

Lucy Sallick, great granddaughter of Titanic passenger Percival White, Sr. (interview with author).

Sealed Orders, By Helen Churchill Candee, originally published in *Collier's Weekly*, May 4, 1912.

The Sinking of the S. S. Titanic, by John B. Thayer, privately published, 1940.

Sinking of the Titanic and Great Sea Disasters, edited by Logan Marshall.

Fred Spencer, Cushing's Island, Maine (emails to author).

State of Maine, Department of Vital Statistics.

The Story of Mount Desert Island, Maine, by Samuel Eliot Morison, An Atlantic Monthly Press Book, Little, Brown and Company, Boston, Toronto.

A Summering Place, by Allan Smallidge.

Titanic: The Canadian Story, by Alan Hustak, Vehicule Press, 1988.

The Titanic: End of a Dream, by Wyn Craig Wade, Rawson, Wade Publishers, New York.

Titanic Survivor, by Violet Jessop, edited by John Maxtone-Graham, Sheridan House, Inc., Dobbs Ferry, New York, 1997.

To Passengers: To Your Scattered Fates, Go!, by Helen Churchill Candee.

U. S. District Court, Southern District of New York.

United States Senate Hearings.

The Winchedon Courier (newspaper).

Winter Harbor Historical Society.

Women Wage Earners: Portland 21st Annual Report of the Bureau of Industrial and Labor Statistics for the State of Maine, Augusta, 1907, compiled by Eva L. Shorey and Elsie Clark Nutt.